ISLAMIC SUFISM IN THE WEST

Islamic Sufism in the West

Moroccan Sufi Influence in Britain:
the Habibiyya Darqawiyya Order as an Example

Dr. Aziz El Kobaiti Idrissi

DIWAN PRESS

Classical and Contemporary Books on Islam and Sufism

Copyright © Aziz El Kobaiti Idrissi, 2013 CE/1434 AH

Islamic Sufism in the West

Published by:	Diwan Press Ltd.
	6 Terrace Walk,
	Norwich
	NR1 3JD
	UK
Website:	www.diwanpress.com
E-mail:	info@diwanpress.com

All rights reserved. No part of this publication may be reproduced, stored in any retrieval system or transmitted in any form or by any means, electronic, mechanical, photocopying, recording or otherwise without the prior permission of the publishers.

Author:	Dr. Aziz El Kobaiti Idrissi
Translation:	Aisha Bewley
Typesetting & cover design by:	Abdassamad Clarke

A catalogue record of this book is available from the British Library.

ISBN-13:	978-1-908892-07-2 (paperback)
	978-1-908892-08-9 (epub)
	978-1-908892-09-6 (Kindle)

Printed and bound by:	Lightning Source

Contents

PREFACE
By Marcia Hermansen — xi

INTRODUCTION
GLOBALIZATION, LOCALIZATION, AND SUFISM
By Mark Sedgwick — xiii

INTRODUCTION
By 'Abd al-Wahhab al-Filali — xix

AUTHOR'S PREFACE — 1

AUTHOR'S INTRODUCTION — 9

Section One
Islamic Sufism in the West — 15

CHAPTER ONE
THE HISTORY OF ISLAMIC SUFISM
IN THE WEST: ITS VARIETIES
AND MODERN BEGINNINGS — 17
Introduction — 17

TOPIC ONE
THE HISTORICAL PRESENCE OF SUFISM IN THE WEST — 18
1. Its intellectual and philosophical presence — 18
2. Its presence through some *tariqa* orders — 19

TOPIC TWO
CATEGORIES OF SUFISM IN THE WEST — 20
1. Works of Western scholars — 20

2. The categories relied on in the study	22
A. Eastern Islamic Sufi orders	23
B. Western Sufi Islamic Orders	23

TOPIC THREE
THE FIRST BEGINNINGS OF ISLAMIC SUFISM IN THE WEST	24
1. A Shaky beginning: Isabelle Eberhardt and the Qadiri order	25
2. A Problematic Indian beginning: Inayat Khan and the Sufi order	26
A. The Sufi Order of Inayat Khan	26
B. The life of Inayat Khan	27
C. The universal message of the Sufi Order	30
D. Inayat Khan and Islam	32
SHAJARA OR (SPIRITUAL LINEAGE) OF PIR-O-MURSHID INAYAT KHAN	35

CHAPTER TWO
THE SHADHILI SUFI TARIQAS IN THE WEST — 37

TOPIC ONE
THE 'ALAWIYYA DARQAWIYYA SHADHILIYYA ORDER	37
1. The Algerian branch of the Moroccan source	37
2. The arrival of the 'Alawiyya order in the West: a historical view	39
3. The Western branch of the order:	42
A. Beginning of its foundation	42
B. The beginning of the split: René Guénon and Frithof Schuon	44
Shaykh Mustafa (Michel Vâlsan)	44
4. The 'Alawiyya Order's Pioneers in the West	45
A. René Guénon	45
Personality	46
His Books	48
B. Frithjof Schuon	49
His Life	49

Contents

His books	51
C. Martin Lings	52
The Phenomenon	52
His life	53
His books	55
D. Titus Burckhardt	56
His Life	56
His books	57

TOPIC TWO
OTHER SHADHILI ORDERS 58
1. The Hashimiyya Darqawiyya Shadhiliyya Order 58
   A. Foreword 58
   B. The Life of its Shaykh 58
   C. His Sufic teachings 60
   D. His works and writings 61
2. The Battawiyya Shadhiliyya Order 61
   A. The life of its Shaykh and his teachings 61
   B. His books 62
3. The Habibiyya Darqawiyya Shadhiliyya order 63
   A. General view 63
   B. The teachings of the Habibiyya order 63

Section Two
The Moroccan Influence in Britain: Through the Model of the Habibiyya Darqawiyya Order   65

CHAPTER ONE
THE HABIBIYYA DARQAWIYYA ORDER 67
Foreword 67

TOPIC ONE
THE MOROCCAN HABIBIYYA DARQAWIYYA ORDER 69
1. General foreword 69
Who was this shaykh? 70

2. Shaykh Muhammad ibn al-Habib ad-Darqawi	70
His noble lineage	70
His birth and primary education	71
His teachings	71
His journeys and his ijazas	72
His works	72
His Sufism	72

TOPIC TWO
THE WESTERN HABIBIYYA DARQAWIYYA ORDER	74
1. Foreword	74
2. Shaykh Abdalqadir as-Sufi al-Murabit "Ian Dallas"	74
A. Biography	74
Chain of isnad chart	77

TOPIC THREE: THE PATH FOLLOWED BY THE WESTERN HABIBIYYA ORDER AND ITS TRANSFORMATION INTO THE WORLDWIDE MURABITUN MOVEMENT	78
1. The path of the Western Habibiyya order	78
2. The Murabitun and reform activities	78
3. Controversial areas	79
A. Dealings with banks and financial activity	79
B. Positions on politics and creed	80

TOPIC FOUR: THE BRANCHES OF THE WESTERN HABIBIYYA DARQAWIYA ORDER	82
1. The Shadhiliyya Haydariyya order of Fadhlalla Haeri	82
A. Foreword	82
B. The life of Shaykh Fadhlalla Haeri	84
C. His works and books	84
2. The Group of Shaykh Mark Hanson (Hamza Yusuf)	85
A. Foreword	85
B. The life of Shaykh Mark Hanson (Hamza Yusuf)	85
C. His works and books	87
Among his translations:	88

CHAPTER TWO

Contents

MOROCCAN INFLUENCE IN BRITAIN: THE WESTERN HABIBIYYA DARQAWIYYA ORDER AS A MODEL   89
Foreword   89

TOPIC ONE
THE MOROCCAN SUFI INFLUENCE ON THE WESTERN HABIBIYYA DARAQWIYYA ORDER   90
1. The *Jalali* (majestic) path   90
    A. The principles of Sufi reflection   90
    B. Manifestations of the *jalali* form   91
2. The *jamali* (beautiful) path   92
    A. The Sira of the Prophet ﷺ   92
    B. **Sama'** and praise   94
    C. Literature and output   95

TOPIC TWO
THE MOROCCAN INFLUENCE ON THE *FIQH*, THEOLOGY AND POLITICS OF THE HABIBIYYA ORDER   96
1. Maliki *fiqh*   96
    A. The special quality of the Moroccan *madhhab*   96
    B. The school of the practice (*'amal*) of the people of Madina   98
2. Political Reform   100
    A. The Murabitun state as a model   100
    B. The personality of the judge: Qadi 'Iyad as a model   101
3. The Ash'ari creed   103
    A. The special quality of the Moroccan creed   103
    B. The **kalam** position of the western Habibiyya order   104

CONCLUSION   107

APPENDICES   109
1. Arabic copy of letter of Shaykh 'Adda ben Tunis   109
2. Chart of the names of the main Sufis mentioned   110
3. Chart of Moroccan texts translated and published by the Habibiyya   111
4. Chart of silsila of Shaykh Abdalqadir   114

5. Chart of silsila of Inayat Khan — 115

Bibliography — 117
1. ARABIC BIBLIOGRAPHY — 119
2. ENGLISH BIBLIOGRAPHY — 123
3. FRENCH BIBLIOGRAPHY — 127
4. WEBSITES — 128

PREFACE

BY MARCIA HERMANSEN[1]

THIS STUDY REPRESENTS the entry of a new and capable researcher into the field of Sufism in the West. Sufism, the mystical interpretation and practice of Islam, is well known in its traditional Muslim homelands and is practised and studied devotionally by Sufis themselves and academically researched by scholars in local environments and languages. In the present book we find the first extended study in Arabic of certain contemporary transnational Sufi movements that represent new ventures in inter-civilizational dialogue and engagement.

Sufi ideas became known in the Western world during the colonial period through translations and interpretations of Sufi poetry and thought, often taken out of an Islamic context. During the 20th century, beginning slowly, Sufi practitioners arrived in Europe and America due to increased access to travel. At the same time, a few intrepid Europeans, known and unknown, journeyed to Muslim lands, embraced Islam and followed Sufi teachers.

In the aftermath of the Second World War, larger waves of Muslim immigrants arrived in Europe and the United States from the Arab countries and South Asia in search of educational and employment opportunities. Among them were Sufis, so that a new emergence of Islamic Sufi Orders (*turuq*) in the West took place. These Sufi Orders taking root in Western soil have included Shadhilis, Naqshbandis, Chishtis, Helveti-Jerrahis, and Qadiris, among others. In order to engage the local societies, Sufi practices and interpretations were also modified to adapt in the new western environment.

---

[1] Professor Dr. Marcia Hermansen, Director of Islamic World Studies Program – Loyola University Chicago, US.

The work of Mr. Aziz Idrissi El Kobaiti is the first study written in Arabic to review and interpret the growing body of Western scholarship on this phenomenon. In it he also uses original sources produced within Sufi movements themselves. What is striking about the present work is its exploration of Sufi networks and discourses in cyberspace, both in terms of tracing archival sources, documents, and photographs, and in following currents and linkages that transcend borders.

An important and original contribution of his work is its focus on influences of the Shadhiliyya Order in the West including intellectual contributions to the study of Islam, such as translations from Arabic and cultural popularization of Sufi writings and practices. Due to its strong historical presence in Morocco, this connection to the Shadhiliyya and in particular to the Habibiyya Darqawiyya branch of the *tariqa*, will certainly interest Maghrebi readers of this work. As Mr. Kobaiti correctly observes, their contributions in the West have had both "*jamali*" and "*jalali*" characteristics, ranging from their promoting devotional practices and appreciation for the artistic heritage of Islamic civilization (*jamali*) to their aspiring to impact political trends (*jalali*).

In situating this study, the Qur'anic verse "*neither of the East nor of the West*" comes to mind, both in terms of the transnational range of the ideas and individuals studied, and the global space in cultural studies that this work occupies.

We felicitate the author and his academic advisors in Morocco for sustaining this important and original project.

Professor Dr. Marcia Hermansen,
Director, Islamic World Studies Program
Loyola University Chicago

INTRODUCTION

GLOBALIZATION, LOCALIZATION, AND SUFISM

BY MARK SEDGWICK[2]

GLOBALIZATION IS USUALLY understood as a one-way process bringing Western cultural influence to the Arab world, and is often resisted or regretted. In fact, although there are certainly problems associated with globalization, it is less of a one-way process than is thought, and is also perhaps less threatening. It is less one-way because, as this book shows so clearly, there has also been Arab and Islamic cultural influence on the West, most notably in the form of Sufi orders and movements. It is less threatening because there is a corollary to globalization that is often forgotten by scholars and intellectuals, but is of real importance: localization.

Global commercial enterprises know all about localization. When a product has been developed for the global market, it must then be localized for local markets before it goes on sale in them. Sometimes this is simply a question of translating the user interface of a computer program such as Windows into local languages. Sometimes it is more complicated, as when McDonalds had to develop "McArabia Grilled Kofta" for the Gulf and Saudi markets (it is not on sale in America). And sometimes localization just happens anyhow, as when the customers eating McArabia Grilled Kofta in a Cairo McDonalds are well dressed, polite, and enjoying their treat. Customers in a "real" American McDonalds are

---

[2] Mark Sedgwick, previously an associate professor at the American University in Cairo, is a professor in the Faculty of Arts at the University of Aarhus and author of *Against the Modern World* and many other books about Islam and Sufism.

rarely well dressed or polite, and never seem to be enjoying themselves very much. They have a very different socio-economic profile, for a start. The main point, though, is that even that great symbol of globalization and American cultural dominance, McDonalds, has been Egyptianized, not because the McDonalds management decided this should happen, but because the power of the local culture is such that it will – to some extent – localize anything that arrives from elsewhere.

Sufism was one of the earliest examples of both globalization and localization. It might be argued that Sufism has been global since at least the thirteenth century CE, when Shaykh Abu'l-Hasan al-Shadhili moved from Morocco to Egypt. More precisely, however, the life of Shaykh Abu'l-Hasan al-Shadhili represents movement within a regional system rather than a global one. Morocco and Egypt were both part of a single regional Islamic system, in which the high culture of the ulema and of the believers was remarkably uniform. Within a regional system such as this, there is not much scope for, or need for, localization.

At much the same time, however, less famous Arab shaykhs were traveling into a different regional system, that of Indonesia, bringing Sufism and Islam itself with them. This was true globalization, since it involved two different regional systems. As a result, Indonesian Islam is in some ways a localized form of Islam. In this context, the word used for "localization" by ulema of the time was less neutral: *bid'a*. *Bid'a* was of course resisted – a more difficult task in Indonesia than in Egypt or Morocco. There were, however, ulema and shaykhs who were either from the Arab world or from the high Islamic tradition, well equipped to undertake this task. Two hundred years later, as Islam and Sufism arrived in south-eastern Europe from Bosnia up to Budapest (at least until the Ottomans lost their Hungarian lands), other ulema and shaykhs performed a similar task

Five hundred years later than this, at the start of the nineteenth century CE, Sufism traveled to Western Europe, but without any Sufi shaykhs or learned ulema to accompany it. Sufism arrived in written form, as reflected in the poetry of Muhammad Shams al-Din Hafiz (1325-89 CE), translated into German by Joseph von Hammer-Purgstall (1774-1856 CE), an imperial Austrian diplomat and scholar who had read these poems

Introduction by: Mark Sedgwick

while on a mission to the Ottoman court between 1799 and 1807. Von Hammer-Purgstall published *Der Diwan von Muhammad Schemsed-Din Hafis, Aus dem Persischen zum erstenmal ganz übersetzt* (The diwan of Muhammad Shams al-Din Hafiz, translated for the first time entirely from Persian) in two volumes, one in 1812 and one in 1813. The German public of the time loved it. Germany's greatest poet, Johann Wolfgang von Goethe (1749-1832 CE), loved it so much that he published his own *West-ostlichen Diwan* (Western-Eastern Diwan) in 1819.

In this volume, Goethe wrote:

Und mag die ganze Welt versinken,
Hafis, mit dir, mit dir allein
Will ich wetteifern! Lust und Pein
Sei uns, den Zwillingen, gemein!
Wie du zu lieben und zu trinken,
Das soll mein Stolz, mein Leben sein.

And even if all the world should sink
Hafiz, with you, only with you
Will I compete! Pleasure and pain
Shall be what we twins have in common.
To love like you, to drink like you –
This is my pride, my life.

Almost a hundred years after Goethe wrote these lines, the Western public seems still to agree with him. Hafiz is now one of the top ten best-selling poets in America, beaten – however – by Jalal al-Din Rumi (1207-73 CE). Rumi is extraordinarily successful in America. In 2006, the various different collections of his poetry and books about his life and teaching were joined by *A Year with Rumi: Daily Readings*, which provides one poem on a page of its own for each day of the year. Millions of Americans have bought this and other such books. Only very, very few of them are Muslim, however.

Rumi has been localized in two ways. Most obviously, he has been translated into English (as well as into less major languages, such as Danish, spoken by only five million people), and packaged and promoted by the Western publishing industry. Less obviously, he is being read by Westerners in ways that he himself could never have imagined, so different is the religion and culture of countries such as America and Denmark from that of the Seljuk empire in which Rumi spent most of his life.

Both America and Denmark are Christian countries, but in very different ways. American Christianity varies from fundamentalist Baptists, who believe that Muslims are damned for failing to accept the Lord Jesus, to liberal Unitarians, who do not think that Jesus was divine. There are hardly any fundamentalist Christians in Denmark, but there are some Christians there who do not even think that God Himself is divine. The religious culture of the West is very varied, then. Importantly, much of it has very little to do with any sort of Christianity.

Sociologists of religion who study America and Europe agree that contemporary Western religious culture is characterized by choice and by a distinction between spirituality and religion. Religion is understood by many Americans and most Europeans as something not only distinct from spirituality, but even as something opposed to spirituality. Religion is the rules and structures of the various churches, which many Westerners regard with little enthusiasm, and pay little or no attention to. Spirituality is the individual experience of that which is beyond the merely physical – that which some call "God" but which some do not. In the West, an atheist can be spiritual – in the Western sense of the word "spiritual", of course.

Western spirituality, then, does not follow the teachings of any one Christian church, or even restrict itself to Christianity. Elements drawn from Hinduism, such as the concept of karma, are sometimes more popular than Christian concepts such as sin. Some Westerners believe more in reincarnation than in the Final Judgment, or more in the powers of forests than in the power of prayer. And the word "some" is very important, because (or so the theory goes) everyone is different. Each person puts together their own individual mixture of beliefs and practices, taking what they like from what is available in bookstores and on the internet and in public lectures, leaving what they do not like, and ending up with a personal religious system that is unique and, from

Introduction by: Mark Sedgwick

a theological point of view, sometimes internally rather contradictory.

Not all Westerners are like this, especially in America, but most of those who read Rumi probably are like this. As well as reading Rumi they may go to church once or twice a year, do meditation exercises derived from Zen Buddhism, and believe in the healing power of crystals. What Rumi himself would have thought of this is hard to imagine.

The religious culture into which the Sufism studied in this book came, then, is very different from the religious culture in which it originated. Like the spread of Sufism to Indonesia or of Sufi poetry to America and Denmark, it is a form of globalization – and a form that is often ignored, quite wrongly. An understanding of this form of globalization is necessary for an understanding of globalization itself, and that is one important reason to welcome this book. Like the spread of Sufi poetry before it, the spread of Sufi orders in the West has encountered the phenomenon of localization. The involvement of Sufi orders and Sufi shaykhs means that the localization is less dramatic than it was in the case of the reading of Rumi, since there is a higher degree of control. The localization that did occur, however, is analyzed in this most valuable book, and is a fascinating topic.

It is not the job of a university scholar to make moral judgments, but to provide accurate information and objective analyses in order to spread knowledge and, in the end, to allow others to make moral judgments that are based on fact and informed by understanding. This is a task that this book performs well, and I wish all its readers an interesting journey through it. It tells us something about the modern West, and it tells us something about modernity everywhere as well, because choice and individual spirituality may have as much to do with modernity as they do with the West. In the end, this book may also tell us something about the development of the religion of Islam in the current era.

Aziz El Kobaiti Idrissi is to be thanked and applauded for having written it.

Dr Mark Sedgwick
Aarhus, November 17, 2007.
University of Aarhus in Denmark,
Coordinator of the Arab and Islamic Studies Unit.

INTRODUCTION

BY 'ABD AL-WAHHAB AL-FILALI[3]

SUFISM IS ONE of the essential components of the cultural and intellectual constitution of Morocco and a basic element of Moroccan Islamic cultural identity. It has persisted through history since it arrived in the Maghrib and it is still today one of the tools for moral behavioural and intellectual growth. It utilises advice from the deen and orientation from its legal sources and the watchfulness of its unique scholars. In spite of some occasional scandals, that puts it far away from forms of extremism and excess, and its practitioners hold to the path of justice and moderation in accordance with the Sunni Maliki school, the Ash'arite creed, and Sufism, following the path of Shaykh Abu al-Qasim al-Junayd.

That, very briefly, is the reality of Islamic Sufism in the Maghrib: a Sufism based on education and learning the principles of rectitude in man's connection to his Creator and his connection to his Prophet ﷺ, to his shaykh, and to all of mankind.

There is no doubt that it took the opportunity to spread out from Morocco to the rest of the earth and other peoples. Moroccan Islamic Sufi influence extends from Morocco to Africa south of the Sahara. As a more than adequate example of that, we can cite the example of the Tijaniyya Tariqa. The present circumstances attest to the confirmation of that, as does the abundance of intellectual material and writing about this and other *tariqas* in Morocco and African lands. Similarly the influence of Sufism has spread from Morocco to Europe and the U.S.A where it has been strengthened by its Moroccan Shadhili, Qadiri and Tijani roots. Today someone who studies its quantitative and relative

---

3   Abd al-Wahhab al-Filali, University of Sidi Muhammad ibn 'Abdullah, Faculty of Literature of Human Sciences, Fez – Morocco.

growth will be amazed at the different areas of Europe and America it has reached. Nevertheless there is a significant difference between the way this Moroccan influence has been expressed in writing in its African and Euro/American manifestations.

Several Moroccan studies have now been done dealing with the Moroccan Sufi presence in Africa but very little has been done regarding the existence of Moroccan Sufism in the West. We can now state clearly that there is a lack of Moroccan studies in this field at a time when this Moroccan Sufi presence is on the increase and when the numbers of Western studies on the subject are also multiplying. This also means that a full picture of Moroccan Sufi influence in the West is certainly lacking which is what is needed to furnish a correct opinion and right conclusions about what is taking place.

This book therefore must be placed in the context of this actual situation; its author attempts to examine other efforts which have been made in this field with the purpose of providing a map of Sufi movements which have emanated from Morocco and are presently to be found in the West by identifying the most important organizations of Sufi orders established there at this time.

This book is a professional academic work and can be considered as a preface to a larger project, which the researcher has in mind: to study Moroccan Sufi influence in the modern West in both the Anglo-Saxon and Francophone worlds.

I can only conclude by saying that I pray for him and his fellow researcher to have success and that is not hard for Allah.

'Abd al-Wahhab al-Filali
University of Sidi Muhammad ibn 'Abdullah
Faculty of Literature of Human Sciences, Fes

AUTHOR'S PREFACE

The presence of Islamic Sufism in different parts of the world is clearly a subject worthy of study and investigation. Researchers and academics are interested in different aspects of this phenomenon. For example, we find some who specialise in the study of the Sufi presence in the Islamic West and in al-Andalus, while others are interested in the Middle East and Persia, and still others specialise in the study of Sufism in sub-Saharan Africa. However, the Islamic Sufi presence in the modern West – Europe and the U.S.A. – has not received adequate attention. Indeed, we are almost totally lacking in studies that cover Islamic Sufi influence in Anglo-Saxon or Francophone lands, and we know very little about the development of the Sufi movement in those parts of the world, which I have classified as a new Islamic phenomenon in the West and which Western academics have labelled "Western Sufism". This type of Sufism adapts, to a certain extent, to its new milieu and plays a positive role in improving the image of Islam in the West. It also makes Islamic Sufism a tool for a mutual relationship and actual dialogue between different religions and cultures, despite the inevitable problems which arise concerning identity and assimilation.

This is the basis of our chosen title: *Islamic Sufism in the West: Moroccan Sufi Influence in Britain, taking the Habibiya Darqawiyya order as an Example*, which will deal with the study of the phenomenon of Sufism in the West in its various forms and Islamic categories. It concentrates on Western Sufi orders in general – what is called "Western Sufism" – firstly because it is a new phenomenon worthy of study and represents the direct contact of Islamic Sufism with the West, and secondly because it is a representative model for studying Islamic influence on Western society with all the problems connected with the debate regarding the exchange of influence and the effect this has had. The title of the study contains three principal elements, which I have attempted to deal with briefly in the first section of the book, and this is followed by an in-depth analysis in the second section.

The first element is "Islamic Sufism in the West" to which the first chapter of this study is devoted. It is a historical study dealing with the penetration of Islamic Sufism into the West which, as an intellectual and philosophical presence, began in the Middle Ages. This was brought about by Western contact with Islamic Sufi thought in Andalusia and in the regions of southern and eastern Europe that were subject to Ottoman influence. However, the modern beginnings of the move of Sufism, as a method for teaching and spiritual instruction, to the West, can be traced to the Colonial period and extended from the end of the 19th century to the middle of the 20th, when the West was in direct contact with Islam in all its aspects.

This situation led to Sufism, as the spiritual aspect of Islam, moving to the West, which was collapsing under the burden of its excessive materialism to the depths of spiritual bankruptcy and thirsting for Eastern spirituality, especially in its Islamic guise. The French scholar, Erik Geoffroy, has dealt with this in an essay of his in French which was printed in the magazine *Annales du Patrimoine*, published by the College of Literature and Sciences in the University of Mostaganem in Algeria under the title, "Le Soufisme d'Occident dans le miroir du Soufisme d'Orient". Western colonisation of the Islamic world together with the philosophical ideologies that dominated Europe in the 19th and 20th centuries and led to Christianity losing its hold over the Western mind were essential reasons for Westerners beginning to look to Islamic Sufism as a solution. It was seen as a successful bastion to reinforce them spiritually and intellectually in their struggle to confront the materialist flood which was washing away Western civilisation.

"The one tangible factor," he says, "in the gradual penetration of Sufism in the West was, paradoxically, colonialism… which reached its greatest extent in the 19th century, and coincided with the emergence of a positivist[4]

---

4 Positivism: A trend in bourgeois philosophy which declares natural (empirical) sciences to be the sole source of true knowledge and rejects the cognitive

Author's Preface

ideology and a civilisation which was more mechanistic and materialistic, while at the same time Christianity, especially Catholicism, was either led, or was on an unstoppable course, towards secularisation. In this climate of 'loss of meaning', Westerners began to look into foreign spiritual traditions for a metaphysical regeneration and a source of illumination. Colonialism at least served to put the West into contact with Islam, even if the situation was one of conflict, and Sufism, as the inner dimension of Islam, actually provided an accessible path and true religious succour for some of those Europeans involved in their countries' colonial ventures."[5]

The special quality of flexibility and forbearance which characterises Sufism enables it take on a form which fits in with a new environment. This has led to the West becoming the home of a number of Sufi orders thatt have ceased merely to be representatives of Eastern Sufism and have in fact established themselves as independent Western branches of traditional Eastern *tariqas,* led by Western shaykhs with considerable numbers of Western followers, which have developed a new perspective greatly influenced by various currents of dominant Western thought of the 19th and 20th centuries. A significant example of this is the Western 'Alawiyya Darqawiyya Shadhiliyya order of Frithjof Schuon, which will be singled out for detailed examination in the second part of the first section of this study. Other Western branches of the Shadhiliyya

---

value of philosophical study. Positivism emerged in response to the inability of speculative philosophy (e.g. Classical German Idealism) to solve philosophical problems which had arisen as a result of scientific development. Positivists went to an opposite extreme and rejected theoretical speculation as a means of obtaining knowledge. Positivism declared false and senseless all problems, concepts and propositions of traditional philosophy on being, substances, causes., etc., that could not be solved or verified by experience due to their highly abstract nature. Positivism claims to be a fundamentally new, non-metaphysical ("positive") philosophy, modelled on empirical sciences and providing them with a methodology. Positivism is essentially empiricism brought to its extreme logical consequences in certain respects: inasmuch as any knowledge is empirical knowledge in one form or another, no speculation can be knowledge. Positivism has not escaped the lot of traditional philosophy, since its own propositions (rejection of speculation, phenomenalism, etc.) turned out to be unverifiable by experience and, consequently, metaphysical.

5   Erik Geoffroy, "Le Soufisme d'Occident dans le Miroir du Soufisme d'Orient" dans: Annales du Patrimoine, n.04, Septembre 2005 p.23

tariqa were also formed, such as the Hashimiyya Shadhiliyya order, the Bitawiyya order and the Habibiyya Darqawiyya order, and these will be the final focus of this section of the study.

The Habibiyya Darqawiyya order is the second element in our title and this means that the first section of the second chapter of this study is devoted to it. Its Moroccan and foreign shaykhs are identified and the form its ideas, principles, methods and influences have taken in its new Western environment are studied and analysed, while note is taken of the different reactions to it in the Western world, both those of support and hostility. Then we devote the second section of the second chapter, the last of the book, to studying Moroccan Sufi influence in Britain, inasmuch as it constitutes a model for what I originally set out to study at the beginning of my research project: the phenomenon of Sufi orders as they have manifested themselves in the West, or what can be technically called "Western Sufism".

So the nub of this study is in fact "Moroccan Sufi influence in Britain" as it is disclosed through the model of the Habibiyya Darqawiyya order, which has a strong presence throughout the West but in particular in Britain. This is by virtue of the fact that its present shaykh, Ian Dallas or Abdalqadir as-Sufi, is Scottish and because the impetus for much of the outward expansion of the Habibiyya order in the West came from the British city of Norwich, due to the presence in it of some of the most prominent followers of the order and the organisational and *da'wa* role it has played in spreading the *tariqa* throughout Britain and the world.

The Western Sufi presence has manifested itself in the model of the Western Habibiyya Darqawiyya order in both a *jalali* way, through its embodiment of Moroccan Sufi teachings and principles taken from Moroccan Sufi texts translated into English by publishing houses connected to the order, and also in a *jamali* way, since Moroccan Sufism concentrates greatly on the life of the Prophet ﷺ and has a strong attachment to the person of the Noble Messenger ﷺ which is expressed by the order through the singing of praises and other forms of *sama'* conducted in the Moroccan style with the behaviour appropriate to it and with innovation that is in harmony with its tradition.

Moroccan Sufi influence in the Western Habibiyya order, which

Author's Preface

spread in Britain, also manifests itself in the matter of belief and legal practice through Ash'ari *'aqida* and Maliki *fiqh*, which are considered to be among the most important distinguishing marks of Moroccan Sufism. The researcher Muhammad Hajji said in this context: "The Moroccans chose the Sufism of Imam al-Junayd, based on good character and *suluk*, as they chose the Ash'ari creed in *tawhid*, and the school of Malik in law. This choice itself is one of the distinguishing qualities of Moroccan Sufism since Moroccan Sufism did not involve itself in the study of spiritual realities, complex epiphanies, ecstatic utterances or the 'unity of existence', except in the case of a very small group."[6]

The goal of studying the subject of Islamic Sufism in the West, and examining the Anglo-Saxon mind by clarifying the influence of Moroccan Sufism on it, is very difficult to achieve. This difficulty is magnified by the absence of Arabic sources in this field, which makes it necessary to depend on Western books alone, and on the beliefs and material and spiritual impulses behind those sources, whose contents must be translated in order for the goal to be achieved. It is proper to mention in this context that all the translated quotations and extracts found in this book are basically down to the personal efforts of the researcher, since, as we have said, there are almost no Arabic sources on the subject. The difficulty of the study is also magnified by the need to follow the methodology adopted by Western researchers, which involves a very cautious and precise approach to identification and investigation and which has as its object the avoidance of bias, a bias which it would be all too easy to fall into if one adhered blindly to the methodologies and writings connected to forms of Islamic Sufism prevalent in the West. The subject demands scholarly boldness, to the point of outright audacity, when dealing with some prominent Sufi ideas in the West which are often in conflict with the Islamic Shari'a.

Notwithstanding these handicaps, this work still hopes to highlight some of the major characteristics of the phenomenon of "Western Sufism" in an authentic scholarly way. It is one of the first comprehensive academic studies in Arabic to set out the history of Islamic Sufism in the

---

6   Hajji, Muhammad. interviewed by: Al-Ishara Newspaper, 2nd year, Vol.16 (April: 2001), p.4

modern West and to identify its best-known leaders from a cross section of Islamic Sufi orders representing the mosaic of the Sufi movement in the West. It is backed up by a substantial collection of documents and rare photographs relating to the development of Islamic Sufi movements and their leaders in the West.

The study covers the whole time period of the subject under discussion by referring to sources extending from the beginning of the 20th century to the present day. I have made use of Inayat Khan's book, *Inner Life*, first published in 1923, and also of modern studies carried out post 2000, such as the study of "European Neo-Sufi Movements in the Interwar Period" by Mark Sedgwick published at the end of 2008. My book attempts to fill a gap, particularly in the field of Moroccan studies of the Anglo-Saxon world, by confirming the existence of the influence of Moroccan Sufism within it, especially in Britain, and by its in-depth study of the influence, in various parts of the world, of the Moroccan Habibiyya Darqawiyya order through its western branch which at a certain point changed into the Worldwide Murabitun Movement.

The whole project has been greatly assisted by access to the Internet. This has had a positive effect on the research needed to accomplish it by enabling links to be forged with other Arab and Western academics working in the area of "Sufism in the West", and with various aspects of the study, such as the informational organisation of the Darqawi Habibiyya order and the World Wisdom site of Frithjof Schuon and his followers. These have provided a great deal of material for this study: important essays, video tapes, photos, events, and other material relevant to the study. I have also been able to gain information about them, read their most recent publications and borrow some items which cannot be found in libraries and national archives, not even in their countries of origin.

My path, however, has been beset by a series of obstacles which I would not have been able to surmount were it not for the help and absolute support, both materially and spiritually, of my professors, particularly those who supervised this study, and their unstinting advice and instruction. I would like to single out for mention Professor Dr. 'Abd al-Wahhab al-Filali, who was my primary support, for his expansive heart and the purity of his precise, methodical, scientific knowledge, and also

Author's Preface

Professor Dr 'Abd ar-Rahim al-'Alami, who was never niggardly with respect to helping me with extra Moroccan sources and who also bore with the bother of midnight phone-calls seeking his advice or the solution to a problem in the book which was preventing me from sleeping.

My thanks are also due to my professor, Ahmad al-Ghazzali al-Yahyawi, who provided me with an excellent means of access to a group of teachers and private organisations expert in the field covered by this study. In this respect I must also acknowledge my recognition of, and indebtedness to, the American professor in the university of Aarhus in Denmark, Dr. Mark Sedgwick, who exchanged information, opinions and documents with me with great openness and integrity, and also the American scholar, Dr. Marcia Hermansen, who gave me access to her most important sources and essays relating to the subject of the study.

This study does not claim to rely on any one specific methodology. Sometimes it deals historically with its subject matter, sometimes it describes it, and sometimes it analyses some of the categories within it; nor does it claim to be comprehensive and to encompass the truth completely. It is simply a starting point which may be correct and may be open to error. It is enough that it opens up a new possibility of dialogue with the West with regard to the study of its ideas on the subject of Islamic Sufism. If my goal in doing this is achieved, then success is from Allah, the Most Merciful, the Ever-Loving; if it is not, it is enough for its author to have had a clear conscience and a good intention in undertaking it.

AUTHOR'S INTRODUCTION

THE FACT OF an Islamic presence in the West is now self-evident and has imposed itself on Western academics despite the attempts of many of them over time to efface it or do away with it. The contemporary French academic Eric Geoffroy says: "Even though the contribution of Islam in shaping the religious and spiritual identity of Europe has obviously waned in the West, as has that of Arab Islamic civilisation in general, Europe is not only the daughter of Greco-Latin culture and Judeo-Christian culture, as we would sometimes like to believe."[7]

The historian R.W. Southern attributes this attenuation and intolerance to the "aversion, ignorance and narrow horizons"[8] of Westerners, especially in men of a religious bias who have played a primary role in sullying the picture of Islam in the West. That is what the two priests, Joseph Cuoq and Louis Gardet, admitted in the book they published under the aegis of the Vatican at the end of Vatican II (1962-1965), when they said: "We must acknowledge with all trust and truthfulness the wrongs which the West has committed and provide evidence to show that we have left behind the ideas and mentality which dominated us in the past. In addition to implementing certain measures now, we need to fundamentally re-evaluate our way of looking at these matters. An essential condition would seem to be to avoid harbouring in our innermost hearts hasty or rash judgements which would appear ludicrous to any sincere Muslim."[9]

---

[7] Geoffroy Eric, "Al-Islam Fi Diyar Urubia" in: Al-Hayat Newspaper, Date 07-06-2009, seen on: http://www.science-islam.net/article.php3?id_article=818&lang=ar

[8] Southern, Richard. *Suratu al-Islam fi Uruba fi al-qurun al-wusta*. Translated by: Redwan Assayyed. House of al-Madar al-Islami. 2nd edition (2006), p.15

[9] Ibid. p.11

There are many reasons for this hostility and intolerance. Principal among them is the fact that Islam has, in fact, always had a strong presence in the West, starting in the Middle Ages when it included southern Europe, especially the Iberian peninsula, and also the great majority of the Balkans in eastern Europe: "We should first recall that the physical presence of Islam in our continent is ancient and deep. It is well known that Spain remained Muslim for almost eight centuries. It is less well known that the same applied to Sicily for four centuries – Palermo had three hundred mosques in the tenth century – and to a lesser extent to southern Italy. In these areas, the lamps of Arab-Islamic culture were not extinguished after the departure of the Arabs but continued to shine for several centuries. And Eastern Europe has had a vast experience of Islam because, due to the expansion of the Ottoman empire, it has been established in the Balkans since the end of the fourteenth century. The centuries of Ottoman rule left a mark which has remained visibly apparent up to the present day."[10]

This presence has not ceased throughout the centuries. Indeed, even today, its effects are deeply felt. "In Kosovo and Albania, for example, we find that Muslims make up 90% of the population in the former and 70% in the latter and, as for Russia, it has known Islam since the eleventh century."[11] And this Islamic presence is also acknowledged by the American academic David Westerlund who says: "During certain periods of time the presence of Islam has been strongly felt in southern Europe. This applies in particular to the Iberian peninsula in the Middle Ages and the Balkans under Ottoman rule. Even now, in the early 2000s, there are high numbers of Muslims in countries of south-eastern Europe, especially in Albania and Bosnia. In some southern parts of Russia, Islam has a long and important history too."[12]

The states of Western Europe, however, did not experience the direct presence of Islam until the period of colonial expansion. This led to the development of a two-way emigration process, by which Westerners

10   Geoffroy Eric, "Al-Islam Fi Diyar Urubia", op. cit.

11   Ibid.

12   David Westerlund, *Sufism in Europe and North America* edit: David Westerlund, 2004 Routledge Curzon, London & New York, p.13

Author's Introduction

who lived in Islamic lands became influenced by the religious life of Muslims in those lands and by which the effects of Islam began to be felt in western Europe, as colonised Muslims emigrated to the West, taking their religion with them. This has had an inevitable effect on their new environment, in which Islam has now become firmly established at the hands of the children and grandchildren of the original emigrants who have become European citizens.

In this context, the scholar Eric Geoffroy has said: "Colonialism led to the development of a great movement of emigration from Europe to the Islamic world. It was followed by direct contact (with Islam) through different waves of emigration in the opposite direction. The most significant of them was the one which took place in the 1960s. At the beginning of the 1980s Islam began to appear in Europe as a true socio-religious presence rather than just a personal or family religion. From that time, a fabric woven from the two social identities (emigrant and European) began to be formed and Muslims began to look openly for places of worship within the European cities where they lived.

"Islam became, especially among the young, a preferred means of gaining a distinct identity, which at the same time enabled them to maintain a personal and social separation within their adopted culture. This re-adaptation of identity, with its religious character, goes along with seeking a more solidly based feeling of belonging in the new environment."[13]

This active growth of Islam in western European countries will lead to the creation of what can technically be called "European Islam" or "Western Islam" and this is the present phase of the Islamic presence in the West. It is, however, a presence with a new and assimilated nature and has taken many and varied shapes due to the connection of Islam, which is a celestial religion born in the East and brimming with spirituality, to the Western world, which is immersed in materialism and no longer has any real ties to religion. So is Western or European Islam a different kind of Islam to its counterpart in the East? Is there a new form of Islam based on geographical, political or racial roots? And, if so, what are the basic premises of this new Islamic presence?

13 Geoffroy, Eric, "Al-Islam Fi Diyar Urubia", op.cit.

"European Islam" was the subject of a research paper given at the International Islamic Conference about "True Islam and its Role in Modern Society," held by the Aal al-Bayt Institute for Islamic Thought in Amman, Jordan, 4-6 July 2005. In it we find: "It is generally accepted that "European Islam", which has necessarily become a recognised reality within European life today due to the fact that it is an integral element of the identity of millions of Muslims who are citizens of European countries, is difficult to define. It has to encompass many national affiliations and sectarian Islamic conflicts and distance itself from concern with any narrow geographical identification because its primary concern is basic Islamic practice. It is not about the problems and difficulties of Muslim lands. It comprehends and lives together with the ideas of Western culture in a spirit of greater tolerance. It strongly inclines towards a rational approach, deals with women and female issues in a more civilized manner, and directs its attention towards political participation and steady work, at least as far as Muslim emigrant affairs are concerned. It believes that different religions and cultures can live together in an atmosphere of tolerance and peace, in a way which adds to social and religious cohesion. 'European Islam' does not strive for the Islamisation of Europe, but is a tool for mutual unification and integration within European society."[14]

I found these to be the tasks facing educated European Muslims who defend the presence of Islam in Europe. Perhaps the Egyptian/Swiss Dr Tariq Ramadan is one of its strongest proponents. In a somewhat less forceful manner we find the scholar Dr. Salah 'Abd ar-Razzaq attempting to explain the idea in a simple way: "What is meant by European Islam is not a geographical or political classification. What is meant by it is a specifically European understanding of Islam. This understanding relies on a combination of realities or facts."[15] These realities and facts refer to the expansion of Islam to far-flung areas of the world, which have customs, usages and traditions unknown to Islam in the past but which, despite these multiple differences, do not fundamentally conflict with Islamic teachings, ideas and rulings.

14 http://www.alkhoei.org/?l=6&b=6&p=37&c=470

15 'Abd Razzak, Salah. "Al Islam al-Urubi" in: Journal of al-Mada, N. 967, (10 June, 2007).

Author's Introduction

He says in explanation: "To a certain extent, Islam has taken on a different aspect in every land to which it has spread, because of the inevitable disparities in national character and the political, social, economic, cultural and historical circumstances it has encountered. That is why some scholars have begun to distinguish between a specific understanding of Islam in one land and a differing understanding in another. This understanding varies according to the social and cultural environment in which it develops and according to the intellectual maturity, cultural development and the nature of the social order in every land where Islam becomes established. In other words, Islam itself remains the same, but the understanding of Islam varies from one environment to another and from one time to another. The principal factor in bringing about the difference is the understanding of Islam, born out of the culture of each land, which inevitably interacts with Islam and gives it its local colour."[16]

Because of this someone who investigates will find that the Iranian understanding of Islam differs from the Moroccan understanding of it and this makes it possible to talk of Iranian Islam, Moroccan Islam, Saudi Islam, Indonesian Islam and Turkish Islam and so on. When the cultural difference is great, it becomes easy to distinguish a specific Islamic form or Islamic understanding. In geographical terms, it simply refers to the cultural environment in which Islam has grown and developed. It does not refer to any political or geographical division based on the political borders of any of these lands. The interaction of Islam with other cultures and civilisations has resulted over the centuries in various flowerings of clearly distinctive Islamic cultural manifestations, so the features of Moghul Islamic culture in India were quite different from the Islamic culture of Ottoman Turkey, and the Islamic culture of Andalusia differed from the African Islamic culture of Timbuktu, Zanzibar and Nigeria.

Salah ibn 'Abd ar-Razzaq concludes by saying: "That is what is now happening through the interaction of Islam with European civilisation: it will result in a 'European Islam', in other words it will produce an Islam with a European colouring, because of the way the Muslims there

---

16 'Abd Razzak, Salah. "Al-Islam al-Urubi" op. cit.

are influenced by the European cultures and societies in which they live. These words may appear strange at the present time, but we have begun to see the development of Islam within the European environment, both among emigrants who live in Europe and Europeans who have embraced Islam."

[17]Similar optimistic appraisals cannot, however, conceal the considerable anxiety which this subject generates. Who can guarantee that Islam will not disappear in Western culture in the same way that Christianity has disappeared? Or that it will not be transformed into a mere personal belief system, unconnected to the concerns of society as a whole – indeed far from the heart of faith itself? Or that the religious identity of Western Muslims will not disappear, once their connections with Islamic countries have been severed, and then this model will be exported back to the East?

Perhaps, therefore, the true focus of any contemporary investigation into the ambivalent relationship between West and East is the touchstone of Islamic Sufism in the West or what has become known as "Western Sufism". This is because some Western scholars have begun to refer to "the Western genius, which has discovered Eastern traditions, absorbed them and in the process changed them and been changed by them."[18] Such a claim, even if true, cannot be totally attributed to "Western genius"; it should rather be largely attributed to the flexibility and power of Islam to adapt itself to different environments, and also to the intellectual openness of traditional Sufism which has enabled it to capture Westerners by its beauty and spiritual appeal and move them from the broken culture of Western materialism to the nobility of the traditional order of Islamic Sufism,

17   Ibid.

18   Andrew Rawlinson, "A History of Western Sufism", Diskus vol.1 no.1, 1993, p.45

Section One

Islamic Sufism in the West

CHAPTER ONE

THE HISTORY OF ISLAMIC SUFISM IN THE WEST: ITS VARIETIES AND MODERN BEGINNINGS

INTRODUCTION

THE PRESENCE OF Sufism in the West today is directly related to the historical presence of Islam there. In the early Middle Ages Islamic Spain gave birth to a group of great Sufis who had a profound influence on other Western Europeans, both Muslim and non-Muslim. This presence continues to be the subject of study and research both in the West and in the Islamic world down to the present time, revealing its intellectual and philosophical aspects rather than the spiritual practices of the *tariqas* within which it flourished and, due to the backward historical and social circumstances prevailing in Western Europe at that period, this led to the study of Islamic philosophy and thought by Western Europeans in order to take benefit from it.

The presence of Sufism as an Islamic spiritual path, containing teaching and spiritual instruction, did not, however, emerge in the West in the form of actual *tariqas* until the colonial period. Islamic Sufism was then able to penetrate the West and recruit followers there who, far from being confined to Eastern emigrants, were, in fact, often from the cream of Western society. They embraced Islam and donned the patched robe of Sufism, thereby establishing a completely new intellectual and religious discipline in the West, which was forced to discard the false picture of Islam that had been built up over the centuries: that it was a reactionary, muddled Messianic heresy, the result of ancient Byzantine corruptions, and other myths and theories about it whose roots went back to the ideas of the ancient Nestorian age.[19] So to Western Sufis belongs the credit of bringing to the West the portrayal of the Islam of the East as one of the great world religions whose creed and Prophetic Message deserve the utmost respect. How did this change come about?

TOPIC ONE
THE HISTORICAL PRESENCE OF SUFISM IN THE WEST

1. ITS INTELLECTUAL AND PHILOSOPHICAL PRESENCE

The influence of Islamic Sufism in the West is not something new. It first began to be felt in the Middle Ages when Europe was enriched by Islamic spirituality stemming from its Sufic source. "Just as there is no doubt that the story of Rabi'a [al-'Adawiyya], the ascetic of Iraq, had a tremendous effect on the court of St. Louis, it is also the case that Sufism nourished the spiritual doctrines of Crusader orders such as the Templars. And it is generally admitted that the work of the Spanish priest Asin Palacios at the beginning of the 20th century showed that North African Sufism had an influence, through spiritual Jews, on the Spanish mystics, St John of the Cross and St Teresa d'Avila. Some Western academics – non-Muslims – have argued that the spiritual exercises of Ignatius of Loyala are also indebted to the methods of Sufi initiation. Was not the Greatest Shaykh of Islamic Sufism, Ibn 'Arabi, (d. 1240) himself born in Spain? Though he later established himself in the East in Damascus, he has now returned to the contemporary West through the spread there of his universal teachings."[20]

Analysis of the various influences and borrowings enables us to demonstrate that Jews, Muslims and Christians often lived in harmony in the territories which came under Muslim rule. If al-Andalus remains the archetype – sometimes idealised – of this peaceful and fruitful

---

19 Southern, Richard. *Suratu al-Islam fi Uruba fi al-qurun al-wusta*, op.cit. p.17

20 Geoffroy Eric, *"Al-Islam Fi Diyar Urubia"*, op.cit.

1. Chapter One: The History of Islamic Sufism in the West

coexistence between the three religions, Asia Minor and the Balkans also saw the birth of a very close inter-relationship, especially between monks and dervishes. In his book, *The Arab Role in the Formation of European Thought*, the scholar 'Abd ar-Rahman Badawi has a section devoted to this influence entitled: "The role of Islamic Sufism in the growth of European Thought".[21] In it he restricts himself to highlighting three definitive instances in which this influence appears: the influence of Ibn 'Abbad ar-Rundi on the great Spanish mystic, St. John of the Cross; the influence of al-Ghazali on Pascal's defence of religion; and then the profound influence of Ibn 'Arabi on the depictions of the Next World by Dante in The Divine Comedy.

2. ITS PRESENCE THROUGH SOME *TARIQA* ORDERS

In the beginning the influence of Islamic Sufism in the West was confined to the intellectual and philosophical domain and did not extend to any direct influence, such as the practices of an actual Sufi *tariqa*.[22] Most contemporary historians of the new Sufi movements in the West believe that such direct influence only became felt in Europe at the end of the 19th and the beginning of the 20th centuries. During that period, due to the particular political, intellectual and religious circumstances prevailing at the time, there was an organic change in European attitudes towards eastern spiritual traditions, especially Islamic Sufism. The French scholar, Eric Geoffroy, attributes this to Christianity's loss of hold over the West due to the spread of the philosophy of positivism, which dominated Europe in the 19th and 20th centuries, and as a result of colonialism which was religiously affected by Islamic Sufism.[23]

In this way branches of a number of great eastern *tariqas* such as the Qadiriyya, Shadhiliyya and Naqshbandiyya began to actively appear in

---

21 Badaoui, 'Abd Rahman. *Dawr al-Arab fi Takwin al-Fikr al-Urubi*. 3rd edition. Leaflets of Printing Agency of Kuwait and House of al-Kalam: Beirut (1979). pp.23-29

22 I exclude here sufi *tariqas* that were under Islamic control in Europe and most of whose followers were Muslim immigrants.

23 Erik Geoffroy, "Le Soufisme d'Occident dans le Miroir du Soufisme d'Orient" dans: Annales du Patrimoine, n.04, Septembre 2005, p.23

the West among emigrants from the East and some Western converts to Islam. Other Westerners came into contact with Islamic Sufism in the East and then returned to the West to form new Islamic Sufi orders along exactly the same lines as the orders in the Islamic world, although differing in their intellectual and philosophical views.

Another group of Westerners with the same goal in mind directed themselves to the study of other Eastern spiritual traditions which led to the appearance in the West of various types of non-Islamic ascetic practices. The name of Sufism was sometimes applied to these, either out of ignorance of the necessary connection between Sufism and Islam or the deliberate denial of this connection, or through the invention, born out of a kind of Western arrogance, of a new spiritual school known as Neo-Sufism, brought about by syncretising various different Eastern spiritual traditions and combining them in the West in a particular way. So the question is: what then actually constitute the different categories of Sufism in the West and what are the basic criteria for making that classification?

TOPIC TWO
CATEGORIES OF SUFISM IN THE WEST

1. WORKS OF WESTERN SCHOLARS

Western scholars divide Sufism into a number of categories on the basis of the application of specific criteria, the most important of which is its connection to the religion of Islam. By example, the professor of religious sciences at the University of Georgia, the American scholar Alan Godlas, divided Sufism in the West into four categories:[24]

1. Islamic Sufi orders in the West
2. Quasi-Islamic Sufi orders or organisations
3. Non-Islamic Sufi orders or organisations
4. Organizations or Schools Related to Sufism or Sufi Orders

The American scholar in the Danish University of Aarhus, Mark Sedgwick, who specialises in Western Sufism, has the same number of categories, but in his case they are different. He says: "It is possible in

---

24 Alan Godlas, "Sufism, the West, and Modernity" in website: http://www.uga.edu/islam/sufismwest.html

1. Chapter One: The History of Islamic Sufism in the West

general to divide Western Sufism into four groups: immigrant *tariqas*, standard *tariqas*, novel *tariqas* and non-Islamic groups."[25]

The immigrant *tariqas* are branches of orders whose roots are spread throughout the Islamic world and which immigrants have brought to the West with them. For the most part, they exist in secret and only attract Muslim immigrants.

The standard *tariqas* are those great orders in the Islamic world which have a number of followers in the West. These orders tend to have Western followers of an original shaykh who remains in the Islamic world. The Budshishi order of Shaykh Hamza al-Qadiri Budshish (b. 1922)[26] and the Naqshbandi order of Muhammad Nazim al-Haqqani (b. 1922) are two leading examples of this type, as they have numerous Western followers and also many immigrant followers among the educated élite who are fluent in the languages of their adopted countries.

The non-Islamic "Sufi" groups are usually personality-based, having grown up around particular individuals. An example of this is the Sufi movement of Idris Shah which quickly transformed into a "Sufism" separate from Islam. Many of its followers are not Muslim and do not consider themselves to have ever been Muslims.[27] Mark Sedgwick categorises any remaining Sufi orders, which are not connected to these three groups, as novel *tariqas*, not known in the Islamic world.

The Professor of Islamic Studies at the Loyola University, Chicago, Marcia Hermansen, has used a horticultural metaphor to describe the presence of Sufism in the West (particularly in the U.S.)[28] and divided them into categories according to their philosophical and intellectual

25 Mark Sedgwick, "Traditionalist Sufism" in Aries 22 (1999), p.4

26 Mark Sedgwick, "In Search of the Counter-Reformation: Anti-Sufi Stereotypes and the Budshishiyya's Response" in: Charles Kurzman and Michael Browers, eds, *An Islamic Reformation?* Lanham, Md: Lexington Books, 2004

27 Mark Sedgwick, "Traditionalist Sufism", op. cit. p.3

28 Marcia Hermansen, "In the Garden of American Sufi Movements: Hybrids and Perennials," in: *New Trends and Developments in the World of Islam*, ed. Peter Clarke, London: Luzac Oriental Press, 1997 pp. 155-178. See also: Marcia Hermansen, "The 'Other' Shadhilis of the West" in *The Shadhiliyya*, ed. Eric Geoffroy, Paris: Maisonneuve et Larose, 2005, pp. 481-499

colouring. They are:

1. Hybrids. This designates orders with an Islamic identity in the West and which stipulate conversion to Islam, holding to Islamic norms, and the fullest possible conformity with the Islamic Shari'a.

2. Perennials. This designates those movements which veil or remove the specific Islamic identity of their Sufism. Most of these movements are those which believe in the "Perennial Philosophy" and "The Religion Perennis" proposed and elaborated by René Guénon, Frithjof Schuon, Ananda Coomaraswamy, Burckhardt and others.

3. Transplants. This designates the groups around teaching Sufi shaykhs from the Islamic world who have moved to the West, particularly the U.S., and who have then formed small circles of *murids* drawn mainly from the immigrant communities.

One reason for the need to specify these groups is that specialist academics have sometimes become confused and fallen into the trap of mixing together Eastern Mysticism in general with Tasawwuf/Sufism which is purely Islamic. Even if something resembling it can be found in ancient religions and cultures, it is not the same. The Swiss scholar, Titus Burckhardt, drew attention to this in his book, *An Introduction to Sufism*, devoting the second section to a discussion of what is meant by Tasawwuf and mysticism, and the link between them, and whether it is permissible to translate the meaning of Tasawwuf as mysticism.[29] In the end, he concludes that Tasawwuf always maintains its essential Islamic characteristics, despite his personal opinion that it is proper to translate Tasawwuf as "Islamic mysticism."

2. THE CATEGORIES RELIED ON IN THE STUDY

In the light of all this I have decided for the purposes of this study to restrict my criteria for the classification of Sufism in the West to the orders which hold to its essential Islamic nature and I have discounted all other types of Western mystic movements which call themselves Sufi. I have also discounted other movements concerned with psychological therapy, which employ some of the tools of Sufism, such as intensive

---

29 Titus Burckhardt, *An Introduction to Sufism*, Translated by D.M. Matheson, Thorsons, an Imprint of Harper Collins Publishers, London (1995), pp.21-30

1. Chapter One: The History of Islamic Sufism in the West

reflection and the repeated invocation of specific Divine names, but which ignore the essential basis of Sufism, its integral connection with the basic religious practices of Islam. Given this, Islamic Sufism is present in the West through two main channels.

A. Eastern Islamic Sufi orders[30]

These are branch orders of major orders based in the Islamic world. They are actively promoted, particularly among immigrants and some Western converts to Islam, and they are many and varied since almost all the orders which exist in the Islamic world are now represented in the West. These orders have emigrated from the Islamic world and are, to a great extent, exact copies of their mother orders in the East. However, educated and politically astute people have subjected these orders to a number of criticisms on the basis of their failure to assimilate and adapt to a Western environment. Exceptions to this rule are some orders which have succeeded in adapting to their Western environment by virtue of the sheer effect of their active presence there along with an effective programme of expansion, as is the case of the Western Budshishiyya order.[31]

B. Western Sufi Islamic Orders

These are Western orders which have become displaced from their Eastern roots and are now overseen by Western shaykhs who adopted Sufism in the Islamic world and then returned to spread it in the West by means of *da'wa* directed basically at Westerners. Such orders differ in their perspectives: the leaders of some have concentrated on teaching Westerners the spirituality of Islam in a form which is easy for them to understand and adapted to their culture; others have run counter to and abandoned the traditional Sufi form they inherited, presenting it as "Traditionialist" philosophy, and have replaced it with a more

---

30 The East here is used in its broader sense which includes countries of the other side of Europe from Morocco, the Middle East to the Far East.

31 Mark Sedgwick, "In Search of the Counter-Reformation: Anti-Sufi Stereotypes and the Budshishiyya's Response" in: Charles Kurzman and Michael Browers, eds, *An Islamic Reformation?* Lanham, Md: Lexington Books, 2004

"modern" approach, "Universalism", which unifies all faiths, believing in the validity of the teachings of all of them down to the present time. This category is, in turn, divided into disparate branches, some of which have basic precepts which make even their Islamic identity subject to doubt and denial. However, the fact that their shaykhs are unanimous in their affirmation of Islam and belief in the Prophethood of Muhammad ﷺ and the truth of the Qur'anic revelation makes me categorise them as Islamic.

Because of the importance of the second type, this section is devoted to studying and analysing it as a new phenomenon, which merits research because of its effect on the question of Sufi identity in the West. So how did Islamic Sufism enter the West. How did it develop its Western character? How much influence of Eastern Islam is there within it? Who are its greatest practitioners? What lies behind the divergences we find in its basic aims?

TOPIC THREE
THE FIRST BEGINNINGS OF ISLAMIC SUFISM IN THE WEST

Perhaps the first to attempt a history of the new phenomenon of Sufism in the West was that of the English scholar Andrew Rawlinson in his treatise entitled *A History of Western Sufism* which deals with the earliest beginnings of the involvement of Westerners in Islamic Sufism. A number of different paths by which it occurred are mentioned. One was at the hands of a Muslim Indian Sufi of the Chishti order and another through the North African Western Shadhili order. Rawlinson says: "In fact, Western Sufism began by adopting two clearly distinct forms which were practically opposites. One of them, the 'Sufi Order', was brought to the West by an Indian Sufi of the Chishti Order, Pir-O-Murshid Hazrat Inayat Khan, ... the other consisted of Westerners in the Shadhili Order and its sub-branches in Egypt, Algeria and Morocco."[32] However, it started with the Qadiri order.

---

32   Andrew Rawlinson, "A History of Western Sufism", Diskus, op. cit., p.54

1. Chapter One: The History of Islamic Sufism in the West

1. A SHAKY BEGINNING: ISABELLE EBERHARDT AND THE QADIRI ORDER

Rawlinson explains: "The first active contact with Sufism – and by 'active' I mean with the intention of following Sufism – came in North Africa. In 1900, Isabelle Eberhardt, an extraordinary Russian better known as a pioneering explorer, was initiated into the Qadiri Order in Tunisia at the age of 23. But this was an isolated initiation, unconnected with any Sufi community, and I think we have to regard it as an exception, made by a Qadiri sheikh who was impressed by Eberhardt and wanted to show her some favour. In any case, nothing came of her initiation; she died four years later, drowned in a flash flood."[33]

The whole question of Isabelle Eberhardt's Islam and Sufism is in fact a matter of some doubt and uncertainty in the eyes of some scholars, one of whom is the American Mark Sedgwick who says: "It is not clear whether Eberhardt observed the Shari'a in other respects... the ritual prayer, periodic fasting, almsgiving and the like... there are no reliable reports of whether or not Eberhardt prayed and fasted."[34] Furthermore her whole outlook was Western: "...dressing not only as a man but as an Arab man, smoking hashish, appearing drunk in public and sleeping with large numbers of Algerian men."[35]

If these claims are true, then the Sufism of Eberhardt and her Islam, which she openly proclaimed in the Western environment, were nothing more than a political stance adopted to counter French colonialism, which she distanced herself from in Algeria. It was simply a device by which she wanted to bring more attention to herself.

The first voice speaking the language of Sufism really directed to Westerners, not by way of being a passing fancy or a political stance but rather as a new beginning and a means of achieving harmony between the body and spirit, was that emanating from the 'Sufi Order', the voice of the Indian Muslim, Hazrat Inayat Khan.

33 Ibid.

34 Mark Sedgwick, *Against the Modern World: Traditionalism and the Secret Intellectual History of the Twentieth Century*, Oxford University Press, 2004, p. 64

35 Mark Sedgwick, *Against the Modern World: Traditionalism and the Secret Intellectual History of the Twentieth Century*, op. cit., p.63

2. A PROBLEMATIC INDIAN BEGINNING: INAYAT KHAN AND THE SUFI ORDER

A. The Sufi Order of Inayat Khan

Most historians of Western Sufism believe that Inayat Khan was one of the first of the new Sufi practitioners to come to the West who directed his spiritual message not only to emigrants there but also to indigenous Westerners.[36] Despite the fact that Inayat Khan came from a Muslim family, the Sufism he offered to the West was in a certain way alien to the standard Sufism predominant in the Islamic World bwcause of the fact that he believed in the universality of Sufism – that Sufism embodied a single inner religious reality which all religions have in common in spite of the outward differences they display. "The greatest work of Inayat Khan lies in the fact that he brought that philosophical order to the Western World which had only been easy for Muslims to attain. He produced a style to change the method of presenting Sufi ideas to the Western World"[37] and "If an average European today has any acquaintance at all with Sufism, it is most likely to be with the work of Khan and Shah, and perhaps with the poetry of Rumi, interpreted in the light of the Khan/Shah understanding of Sufism."[38]

Even if this understanding differs to some extent from the understanding generally current in the Islamic world, Khan only acted as he did out of a sincere desire to lend a great service to Islam and Islamic Sufism, which only found a fertile land in which to plant its seeds in the West in the wake of the exemplary work of Khan and his efforts to purge the Western mind of its feelings of aggression towards

---

36   Andrew Rawlinson, "A History of Western Sufism", Diskus, op. cit. pp.45-83. See also Mark Sedgwick, "European Neo-Sufi Movements in the Interwar Period" in *Islam in Europe in the Interwar Period: Networks, Status, Challenges*, Nathalie Clayer and Eric Germain, eds., forthcoming, London: Hurst

37   Inayat Khan. *Ta'alim al-Mutassawifin*, translated by: Ibrahim Istanbuli. House of al-Farkad: Syria, Damascus, 1st edition (2006) p.13

38   Mark Sedgwick, "European Neo-Sufi Movements in the Interwar Period" in *Islam in Europe in the Interwar Period: Networks, Status, Challenges*, Nathalie Clayer and Eric Germain, eds., forthcoming, London: Hurst

1. Chapter One: The History of Islamic Sufism in the West

the Message of Islam, its bearer and everything connected to them. Although Khan aspired to transcend all religions with his spiritual teachings, he required his followers and those influenced by him to respect Islam as a Divinely Revealed Religious Message and to respect the Prophet of Islam as a Divinely appointed Messenger.

B. The life of Inayat Khan

Inayat Khan was born in the city of Baroda in Gujarat in India on July 5th 1882. His grandfather, Moula Bakhsh, was a well-known palace musician and the man who established the notation rules of Classical Indian music. Inayat Khan's family were Muslims and at an early age he established the five times of the daily prayer beside the adults. At the age of nine he received a prize from Gaekwar, Maharaja of the city of Baroda, for his singing of religious hymns.[39]

As a young man Inayat achieved great fame as a musician. He travelled throughout the whole of India and it would appear that he was considered the greatest Indian musician of that time. However that did not satisfy the spiritual longing he felt in his innermost being. We find in Inayat Khan's biography: "At nightfall he went home and said *tahajjud*, the midnight prayer. And lo! at the end of his prayers there came to him a voice, as though in answer to his invocations. It was the voice of a *faqir*, calling the people to prayer before sunrise, and he sang: 'Awake, O man, from thy fast sleep! Thou knowest not that death watcheth thee every moment. Thou canst not imagine how great a load thou hast gathered to carry on thy shoulders and how long the journey is yet for thee to accomplish. Up! Up! the night is passed and the sun will soon arise!' The unearthly quiet of the hour and the solemnity of the song moved Inayat to tears. Sitting on his rug with a rosary in his hand, he reflected that all the musical proficiency and reputation which he had achieved were utterly profitless in regard to his salvation". He recognised that the world was neither a stage set up for our amusement nor a bazaar to satisfy our vanity and hunger, but a school wherein to learn a hard lesson. He then chose quite a different path to the track

---

39   Inayat Khan. *Ta'alim al-Mutassawifin*, op. cit., p.9

which he had followed until then, in other words he turned over a new page in his life.[40]

Inayat Khan started to study the Divine wisdom he found in Islamic Sufism, whose aim is to purify the heart and control the self and did not forbid the music which was such a fundamental part of Khan's life. That is because the Sufis consider music to be a means for the soul to achieve the state of divinely inspired bewilderment which occurs when the ego withdraws from the world of duality and attains nearness to Allah. This state is called ecstasy or awe. Inayat had already had direct experience of such Divine ecstasy in which he was a man drowning in a sea of wonderful sounds.

One day he had a dream: he was present at a musical gathering among a group of great Sufis of the distant past when all those present chanted, "Allah is greater. Allah is greater." After he woke up, he continued to hear the music as clearly as he had in his dream and those words, "Allah is greater." That marked his entry into the heart of Sufism.[41] It was the basic step he had to take. After that it became necessary for him to seek a spiritual master who would take his hand as a guide to the inner world and bring him safely to the shore of arrival and salvation.

One day Inayat was sitting in the house of a friend who was also a Sufi. They were having a conversation when the owner of the house suddenly became agitated. He leapt up and quickly began to tidy the room and put the cushions in the place singled out for honoured guests. A short time later a person entered the room whose appearance dazzled Inayat, especially his face. It was the same face which Inayat had seen again and again in his dreams. After he had looked over all those present, the shaykh's glance rested on Inayat and he asked the owner of the house: "Who is this lad?" The owner answered, "He is a musician interested in Sufism but he has been seeking guidance for six months without success." Then the shaykh turned to Inayat Khan and invited him to join the circle of his students immediately. The name of that teacher was Shaykh Sa'id Muhammad Madani, who was from a family of Sharifs. In

---

40   Ibid. p.41
41   Ibid. pp.10-11

1. Chapter One: The History of Islamic Sufism in the West

that way he became the *murshid*, or teacher, of Inayat Khan.[42]

After Inayat had spent several years travelling the path of a *murid* within the Chishti order, his shaykh called him one day to charge him with the task to which he would devote the whole of the rest of his life. Shaykh Madani called him to him and during their conversation alone together he gave him the following instruction: "Fare forth into the world, my child, and harmonize the East and West with the harmony of thy music. Spread the wisdom of Sufism abroad, for to this end thou hast been gifted by Allah, the Compassionate, the Most-Merciful." From that moment Inayat Khan began to follow the instructions of his *murshid* and strove to be the bearer of the Sufi Message, the message of the liberation of the spirit, throughout the world.[43]

In 1910 Khan travelled from India to the U.S. and, after a tour in which he held lectures and musical performances, he moved from America to Europe where he spent the rest of his life. Between 1912 and 1914 Khan travelled to England, France and Russia to hold Indian musical performances and to give lectures on both spirituality and music. A number of his lectures were presented under the auspices of the Theosophical Society who published an English edition of his book, *A Sufi Message of Spiritual Liberty*. The book was also translated into French and Russian.[44]

Inayat was a tireless teacher, writer, and lecturer, travelling and lecturing almost continuously for seventeen years. He established his school in France and had a dedicated group of disciples. However, his gruelling schedule had weakened him over the years. In 1927 he left for India to see his homeland for the first time in seventeen years. He hoped to rest and meditate but was asked to lecture and, as usual, graciously consented to do so. He died of influenza in New Delhi at the age of 44.[45] His tomb is close to the tomb of Nizam ad-Din Awliya and is considered

[42] Ibid. pp.11-12

[43] Ibid. p.12

[44] Inayat Khan, *Biography of Pir-o-Murshid Inayat Khan* (1923) [Germany]: Centrum Universel, 2005; e-book, pp.53-60

[45] "Hazrat Inayat Khan: Founder of the Sufi Order in the West" in website: http://www.om-guru.com/html/saints/khan.html

a place of pilgrimage for Sufis from all parts of the world.

C. The universal message of the Sufi Order

Inayat Khan called his Sufi order "Universal Sufism" and his teachings are known by this name. It is possible that Khan's model, in calling them that, were the teachings of Shaykh al-Akbar Muhyi ad-Deen Ibn 'Arabi, who had a strong influence in the West, particularly in the areas of philosophy and Sufism.[46] He is said to have created the precedent of calling Sufism "universal", a claim also made by the contemporary English scholar, Peter Young in his essay, "Ibn 'Arabi: Towards a Universal Point of View".[47] However, even if Ibn 'Arabi did speak about the universality of Sufism and say that the heart of the Sufi is tolerant and open to all beings, it is because he follows the deen of love, as in his famous verses:

"My heart can take on every form:
pasture for gazelles, a hermitage for the monk,
a house for idols, a Ka'ba for the one who does Tawaf,
the tablets of the Torah and the copy of the Qur'an.
I follow the religion of love. Wherever his mounts turn,
love is my religion and my faith."[48]

It is clear, however, that he understood the practice of Sufism as only being within Islam and thought that absolute perfection was only to be found in the light of the Muhammadan Prophethood. Frithjof Schuon, a Western universal Sufi Muslim, says: "Ibn 'Arabi belonged to the civilization of Islam and owed his spiritual realization to the Islamic *barakah* and the Masters of Sufism, in a word, to the Islamic form of religion; he must needs, therefore, have placed himself at this point of view, that is to say, at the standpoint of the relationship wherein the

---

46   James Winston Morris, "Ibn 'Arabi in the 'Far West' Visible and Invisible Influences" in the Journal of the Muhyiddin Ibn 'Arabi Society, IX (2001), pp.87-122.

47   Peter Young, "Ibn 'Arabi: Towards Universal Point of View" in the Journal of the Muhyiddin Ibn 'Arabi Society, V, (1999), pp.88-97

48   Ibn 'Arabi, Muhyi ad-Din, *Dhakha'ir al-A'laq: Sharh Tarjuman al-Ashwaq*, leaflets of Muhammad Ali Baydoun, House of al-'Ilmiyya, Lebanon: Beirut. 1st edition (2000CE/1420AH), pp.35-36

1. Chapter One: The History of Islamic Sufism in the West

Islamic form is superior by comparison with other forms."[49]

Khan went even further than that and considered Sufism not to be attached to any specific religion because it was above all religions. He clearly states: "Sufism as a school has come from the East to the West, but Sufism as a message is from above the earth, and in that sense Sufism belongs neither to the East nor the West. The Sufi esoteric school has behind it the tradition of the ancient Sufi schools which existed in all past ages, but the Sufi message has its own tradition. It is more than a school: it is life itself; it is the answer to the cry of the whole of humanity."[50]

We find Khan writing for his followers the creed of Universal Sufism which can be summarised in ten foundational principles:

1. There is One God, the Eternal, the Only Being; none exists save Allah.

2. There is One Master, the Guiding Spirit of all souls, Who constantly leads all followers toward the Light.

3. There is One Holy Book, the Sacred Manuscript of Nature, the only Scripture that can enlighten the reader.

4. There is one Religion, the unswerving progress in the right direction, toward the ideal, which fulfils the life purpose of every soul. "The Sufi affirms the one divine wisdom-teaching present in all the Prophetic messages. He sees the same timeless universality in everything in different forms and at different times".[51]

5. There is One Law, the Law of Reciprocity, which can be observed by a selfless conscience, together with a sense of awakened justice.

6. There is one Family, the Human Family, which unites the Children of Earth indiscriminately in the Parenthood of God.

7. There is one Moral Principle, the love which springs forth from self-denial, and blooms in deeds of beneficence.

8. There is one Object of Praise, the Beauty which uplifts the

---

49 Frithjof Schuoun, *Al-Iman, al-Islam Wa al-Ihsan Fi Muqaranati al-Adyan*, translated by: Nihad Khayyata, University Press for Studies, Print and Publication: Beirut. 1st edition (1996CE/1416AH), p.45

50 Inayat Khan, *Ta'alim al-Mutassawifin*, op. cit. p.26

51 Ibid. p.46

heart of its worshipper through all aspects from the seen to the Unseen.

9. There is one Truth, the true knowledge of our being within and without, which is the essence of all wisdom.

10. There is one Path, the annihilation of the false ego in the real, which raises the mortal to immortality and in which resides all perfection.

There is concentration on three basic explanatory points:

1. Universal Sufis believe in the essential unity of the great religions of the world. However, this does not mean they believe that the various religious creeds and doctrines are identical. Rather, they view all religions as having sprung from the same spiritual source.

2. The social and outer forms of different religions vary due to the circumstances at the time that they were founded. Other differences in doctrine and belief can be attributed to later accretions, after the death of the founder.

3. Every person has an immortal soul. Unlike everything else in creation, it is not subject to decomposition. At death, the soul is freed to travel through the spirit world. The latter is viewed as a timeless and placeless extension of our own universe – not some physically remote or removed place.

D. Inayat Khan and Islam

Despite the fact that the teachings of the Sufi order Khan founded have now become a Western departure from the Eastern spiritual tradition on which they were founded, because of the non-Islamic elements they contain, its followers continue to be eager to connect the chain of Khan's spiritual inheritance to the old Sufi order he belonged to in India: the Chishti order which he took directly from his shaykh Sa'id Muhammad Madani. Other sources also indicate that he joined other Islamic Sufi orders, such as the Naqshbandiyya, Qadiriyya and Suhrawardiyya.[52]

The Sufism of Inayat Khan originally did have a genuine, though superficial, connection to traditional Islamic Sufism but it soon began

52   Ibid. p.12

1. Chapter One: The History of Islamic Sufism in the West

to be very different from it. Khan presented Sufism as reflecting that aspect of it which his Indian teacher used to describe as "the essence of all religions and philosophies".[53] This statement became widespread among his followers. The American scholar Mark Sedgwick says about this: "Regular Sufis in the Islamic world would subscribe to this statement to a certain extent: Sufism is for them the quintessence of Islam, and Islam is the quintessence of religion...Khan probably believed something of this privately, but publicly proclaimed something rather different. As a result, for most of Khan's followers, Sufism was not a part of Islam, but something above and beyond Islam."[54]

"Despite this," Sedgwick continues, "Khan's teaching is recognisably Sufic in the classic Islamic fashion. He writes, for example, of the need to subdue the *nafs* (ego) in order to achieve *fana* (spiritual union) in God. ... The path to this is the attainment of purity, a concept which Khan (with little justification) derives from the word 'Sufi'. One variety of purity is to 'make the heart free from all impressions that ... are foreign to one's nature', an idea which is at first rather like Elwell-Sutton's 'prescriptions of self-improvement'. However, what is 'against one's nature' has previously been defined by Khan as a 'fault', and one example of such a 'fault' is 'every rising wave of passion [which inevitably] carries away one's reason.' The need to control the passions to cleanse the heart is a central message of regular Sufism, and is not characteristic of modernist self-improvement."[55]

Khan wrote something similar about the immense implications of "purity". True purity is "preserving the mind of the individual from all other than God. Here all that he thinks or sees or admires or touches or feels becomes God."[56] Is this not Islamic Sufism itself? But he presented

53 Angela Alt, "An Open Letter on Sufism" in: The Sufi, Vol.1, September 1934, p.223

54 Mark Sedgwick "European Neo-Sufi Movements in the Interwar Period" in *Islam in Europe in the Interwar Period: Networks, Status, Challenges*, Nathalie Clayer and Eric Germain, eds., forthcoming, London: Hurst.

55 Mark Sedgwick "European Neo-Sufi Movements in the Interwar Period" in *Islam in Europe in the Interwar Period: Networks, Status, Challenges*, op. cit.

56 Inayat Khan, *The Art of Being and Becoming*, New Lebanon, NY: Omega, 1982, p.10-11

through his stories and statements matters which would attract both the religious and non-religious in the West.

In his autobiography Khan admits that he altered Islamic Sufism so that it would be suitable for contemporary Western consumption. He says: "Western nature is self-assertive and demanding. That is why spiritual attainment becomes difficult for the people in the West, as it is only attained through self-effacement and self-denial. The idea of crushing the I, to become selfless, to become indifferent to the life around one... to feel that one must lose oneself in God and to consider individuality to be an illusion ... these things frighten many away from a deeper understanding of the philosophical thought of the East. Therefore those who have worked in the West in spreading the spiritual thought have to keep back many deep ideas of philosophy in order to deal successfully with the people there."[57]

Khan also perceived "the prejudice against Islam" which he ascribes in a very Muslim fashion to "Christian missionaries" who, knowing that Islam is the only religion which can succeed their faith, have done everything in their power to prejudice the minds of the Western people against it.[58] "As a result, I have always seen that a Western person of good intention who has given up all prejudices against other religions and is trying to overlook all he has heard against Islam, cannot very well comprehend the ideas of the Qur'an as they are put. For he wants the ideas to fit in with the standard of the day and to be expressed in the language of the present time."[59]

Khan affirmed that the message of Islam is the most perfect of all religious messages and so he called people in a direct way, but in an altered form, to join Islamic Sufism, saying: "In each age the message was revealed more and more clearly according to the capacity of the world to bear it; and this went on until the last and clearest Revelation, the Message of Muhammad, the Seal of the Prophets. After this no more Prophets were needed; the world was awakened to the understanding

---

57 Inayat Khan, *Biography of Pir-o-Murshid Inayat Khan*, op. cit., p.164
58 Ibid. p.138
59 Inayat Khan, *Biography of Pir-o-Murshid Inayat Khan*, op. cit., p.136

1. Chapter One: The History of Islamic Sufism in the West

of true reality. This is not the time to wait for the coming of another Prophet; now is the time to awaken to the truth within ourselves. And if there is a friend who has gone this way already, now is the time to ask his advice."[60]

Perhaps an analytical, scholarly study of this matter, dealing with the connection of Inayat Khan to Sufism and tasked with answering the question, will throw some light on the ambiguity and obscurity surrounding his teachings, about which Western thinkers have written in an effort to divest this man of his Islamic identity, with or without the previously mentioned aim. We do not fail to acknowledge some efforts made in this context, but they are slight in comparison with the volume of the output of the man and his ample role in acquainting the West with the wealth of Islamic thought: "If ideas move from a specific cultural environment to another, it is a difficult knowledge which is beyond the capacity of the intellect. For that reason, what Inayat Khan did in transmitting the ideas of Sufism from the West to the East is beyond price."[61]

As well as the efforts of Khan there is also what has been undertaken by followers of the Shadhili Darqawi order in the West, to whom must be ascribed the virtue of achieving a relative compromise between the Muslim East, described as spiritual, and the scientific West, described as materialist. How did this compromise occur? What were the most important active elements in it? What are the stages through which it passed?

SHAJARA OR (SPIRITUAL LINEAGE) OF PIR-O-MURSHID INAYAT KHAN
ALLAH
Hazrat Jibra'il
Hazrat Khwaja Muhammad Rasul Allah
Hazrat Khwaja 'Ali Wali Allah
Hazrat Khwaja Hasan Basri
Hazrat Khwaja 'Abd al-Wahid bin Zayd

---

60   Inayat Khan, *Ta'alim al-Mutassawifin*, op. cit., p. 45
61   Inayat Khan, *Ta'alim al-Mutassawifin*, op. cit., p.13

Hazrat Khwaja Fuzayl bin 'Iyaz
Hazrat Khwaja Ibrahim Adham
Hazrat Khwaja Huzayfa Mar'ishi
Hazrat Khwaja Hubayra Basri
Hazrat Khwaja Mumshad 'Ulu Dinwari
Hazrat Khwaja Abu Ishaq Shami
Hazrat Khwaja Abu Ahmad Abdal Chishti
Hazrat Khwaja Abu Muhammad Chishti
Hazrat Khwaja Abu Yusuf Chishti
Hazrat Khwaja Qutbuddin Mawdud Chishti
Hazrat Khwaja Hajji Sharif Zindani
Hazrat Khwaja 'Usman Harvani
Hazrat Khwaja Mu'inuddin Hasan Sanjari-Ajmiri
Hazrat Khwaja Qutbuddin Mas'ud Bakhtiyar Kaki
Hazrat Khwaja Fariduddin Ganj-i Shakar Ajhodani
Hazrat Khwaja Nizamuddin Mahbub-i Ilahi Badauni
Hazrat Khwaja Nasiruddin Chiragh Dihlavi
Hazrat Shaykh al-Masha'ikh Kamaluddin 'Allama
Hazrat Shaykh al-Masha'ikh Sirajuddin
Hazrat Shaykh al-Masha'ikh 'Ilmuddin
Hazrat Shaykh al-Masha'ikh Mahmud Rajan
Hazrat Shaykh al-Masha'ikh Jamaluddin Jamman
Hazrat Shaykh al-Masha'ikh Hasan Muhammad
Hazrat Shaykh al-Masha'ikh Muhammad A'zam
Hazrat Shaykh al-Masha'ikh Yahya Madani
Hazrat Shaykh al-Masha'ikh Shah Kalim Allah Jahanabadi
Hazrat Shaykh al-Masha'ikh Nizamuddin Awrangabadi
Hazrat Shaykh al-Masha'ikh Maulana Fakhruddin
Hazrat Shaykh al-Masha'ikh Ghulam Qutbuddin
Hazrat Shaykh al-Masha'ikh Nasiruddin Mahmud Kali Shah
Hazrat Shaykh al-Masha'ikh Muhammad Hasan Jili Kalimi
Hazrat Shaykh al-Masha'ikh Muhammad Abu Hashim Madani
Hazrat Pir-o-Murshid Inayat Khan

CHAPTER TWO

THE SHADHILI SUFI TARIQAS IN THE WEST

TOPIC ONE
THE 'ALAWIYYA DARQAWIYYA SHADHILIYYA ORDER

1. THE ALGERIAN BRANCH OF THE MOROCCAN SOURCE

THIS BRANCH OF the Darqawiyya Shadhiliyya order is named after the Algerian Shaykh Ahmad ibn Mustafa called al-'Alawi (Bin 'Aliwa and al-'Alawi by *kunya*), who inherited his secret from the Moroccan Sufi Gnostic, Sidi Muhammad ibn al-Habib al-Buzaydi, who inherited from the Moroccan Sufi Muhammad, ibn Qaddur al-Wakili, who took it from the Moroccan Sufi, Abu Ya'za al-Mahaji, who took it from the great gnostic Shaykh al-'Arabi ad-Darqawi, the founder of the Moroccan Darqawi *tariqa*, which spread to all corners of the world and was very well known in Algeria.

At the end of the 18th century Algeria was a fertile land from the Darqawi point of view, a place where its call would be heard and new *murids* recruited from among its inhabitants discontented with Ottoman rule. The Shadhilis of Algeria began to be known as Darqawis, especially in the west of the country. According to Rinn: "The Darqawis of that order represent the Moroccan branch of the Shadhiliyya. There are many Darqawi Shadhilis in Algeria. Shaykh al-'Arabi (ad-Darqawi) engendered a number of *murids* and shaykhs…. Some of them founded a new order born out of the Darqawi line."[62]

The Moroccan Darqawi influence on Algeria was so strong that on two occasions a number of Algerian Sufis, specifically the Shadhilis and Darqawis, pledged allegiance to the Moroccan Sultan, Moulay Sulayman.[63] Moroccan Sufi influence on the 'Alawiyya order is also evident in the chain of the spiritual descent of Ahmad ibn Mustafa al-'Alawi (b. 1869/1286 and d. 1934/1352), which contained fifteen Moroccan shaykhs with a direct *isnad* to Shaykh Ahmad Zarruq. Before him we find eastern shaykhs but return to Morocco with the Qutb Abu al-Hasan ash-Shadhili and his shaykh, 'Abd as-Salam ibn Mashish.

That is the spring of Darqawi Sufism, at which Shaykh Ahmad ibn Mustafa al-'Alawi drank, and he achieved a great rank in it, making him the focus of a large number of *murids*, not just from the Arab or Islamic world, which would have been enough by itself, but also from Europe and the U.S.A., where his fame spread because of the great openness and flexibility of his teachings and his tolerant and charismatic personality.

The French scholar, Eric Geoffroy, says about him in his essay entitled "Le rayonnement spirituel du cheikh Al-Alawi en Occident": "The influence of Shaykh 'Alawi was such that it affected many Europeans. Whether they were orientalists, converts to Islam or just visitors, all of them stress the personal magnetism that emanated from the Shaykh. Regarding the testimony of orientalists, I will confine myself to just two of them. Arberry, for example, recognized that the sanctity of Sheikh al-'Alawi "recalled the golden age of medieval mystics." Despite that he wrote in the same book, entitled *Sufism*, that there had not been any real mystics since Junayd or Ibn 'Arabi. He first argued that mysticism had declined after the thirteenth century and then stated that there was a contemporary saint worthy of the great medieval masters."

Similarly, Martin Lings [or Abu Bakr Siraj ad-Din), in his book, *What is Sufism?*, compared Shaykh al-'Alawi to al-Junayd of Baghdad, who was named

---

62   Al-Khidari, Muhammad, "Ad-dawr as-siyasi li Tariqa ad-Darqawiya Fi al-'Alaqat bayna al-Maghrib Wa al-Jaza'ir fi Bidayat al-Qarn at-Tasi' 'Ashar" in: al-Manahil Magazine, Az-zawaya Fi al-Maghrib ch.1, p.260

63   Ibid. pp.260-261

1. Chapter Two: The Shadhili Sufi Tariqas in the West

'the master of the order of Sufis'.[64] Martin Lings also described Shaykh Ahmad ibn Mustafa al-'Alawi as "A Sufi Saint of the Twentieth Century" in a book which he wrote in English under the same name.[65] There is also Augustine Berque, the father of the famous French orientalist Jacques Berque who died in 1995. "Augustine Berque spent time with Shaykh al-'Alawi from 1921 until the latter died in 1934. He was fascinated by the character of the shaykh, and even wrote a long article about him. He praised the completeness of the shaykh. He saw in him both a traditional saint and a modern visionary."[66]

The special quality of the contemporary nature, openness, and vision of Shaykh al-'Alawi, coupled with his preservation of his traditional roots, made some élite Western thinkers, such as Frithjof Schuon, accept Sufism at his hand, or send to him all those who desired to drink in this type of Eastern spirituality, as Rene Guenon did. Who were they? What was their connection to Islamic Sufism in general and the 'Alawi Darqawi order in particular? What was their role in establishing the Western branch of the 'Alawi Darqawi Shadhili order?

2. THE ARRIVAL OF THE 'ALAWIYYA ORDER IN THE WEST: A HISTORICAL VIEW

All Western studies which attempt to examine the new phenomenon of Islamic Sufism in Europe indicate that the first Western connection with the Eastern Shadhiliyya which had an effective role in the growth of Western Sufism was the one which took place in Egypt through the Swedish painter Ivan Aguéli,[67] who embraced Islam in 1908 under the

64 http://alalawi.1934.free.fr/modules.php?name=Content&pa=showpage&pid=24

65 Martin Lings, *A Sufi Saint of the Twentieth Century: Shaykh Ahmad al-Alawi, His Spiritual Heritage and Legacy*, ed.3, The Islamic Texts Society, Cambridge(1993).

66 http://alalawi.1934.free.fr/modules.php?name=Content&pa=showpage&pid=24

67 Ivan Aguéli (born John Gustaf Agelii) (May 24, 1869 – October 1, 1917) also named Sheikh 'Abd al-Hadi 'Aqili (Arabic: شيخ عبد الهادى عقيلى) upon his conversion to Islam, was a Swedish wandering Sufi, painter and author. As a devotee of Ibn 'Arabi, his metaphysics applied to the study of Islamic esotericism and its similarities with other esoteric traditions of the world. He was the initiator of René Guénon into Sufism and founder of the Parisian al-Akbariyya society. His art was a unique form of miniature Post-

name 'Abd al-Hadi 'Aqili and who became a Shadhili at the hands of Shaykh 'Abd ar-Rahman 'Illysh al-Kabir. He was the shaykh of a somewhat obscure branch of the Shadhili Order, the 'Arabiyya-Shadhiliyya. This Shaykh appointed Ivan Aguéli as his *muqaddim* in the West, meaning that he had some authority to initiate Westerners into Sufism.

But the definitive point of the introduction of the Eastern Sufi presence in the West can be traced back to the conversion of the French thinker René Guénon to Islam and his joining the Shadhiliyya through Ivan Aguéli in Paris in 1912.[68] As Andrew Rawlinson says:

"So the situation around the outbreak of WW1 is that the Shadhili Order has just two Western members:[69] Aguéli (who has the authority to initiate others) and Guénon (who appears to be the only person he actually did initiate). Agueli died in 1918 and Guénon is a closet Sufi. This is a fragile plant."[70]

In 1930, René Guénon left France and went to Egypt, where he was to spend the rest of his life under his new name, Shaykh 'Abd al-Wahid Yahya. While there he basically stayed in his house, attending some of the gatherings of *dhikr* and reflection held by Shaykh Salama ar-Radi, the shaykh of the Hamidiyya Shadhiliyya order. The scholar Faruq Nasr Mitwalli said in praise of the Shaykh of the Hamidiyya, whose circle Guénon attended: "He was a Sufi philosopher who was able, through the path he laid out for himself, to distinguish himself through careful management, profound faith, true giving, fine words, and skilful debate. He was pre-eminent in all those matters, which made some orientalists eager to attend his gatherings, accept his views, and benefit from his knowledge. One of them was the Frenchman Réné Guénon who became Muslim at his hands, adopting the

---

Impressionism where he used the blend of colours to create a sense of depth and distance. His unique style of art made him one of the founders of the Swedish contemporary art movement.

68 Nasr Mutawalli Wahba, Faruq, *Al 'Arif Billah: Sidi Salama ar-Radi: al-Faylasuf wa as-Sufi wa ash-Sha'ir wa al-Adib*, (Vol.1). 1st edition (1988CE/1409AH).

69 Sedgwick, Mark,"European Neo-Sufi Movements in the Interwar Period" in *Islam in Inter-war Europe*, ed. Nathalie Clayer and Eric Germain (New York: Columbia University Press; London: Hurst, 2008).

70 Andrew Rawlinson, "A History of Western Sufism", Diskus op. cit., pp.45-83

1. Chapter Two: The Shadhili Sufi Tariqas in the West

name 'Abd al-Wahid Yahya. The fact that he was a considerable scholar in Islamic philosophy and Sufism, and his eagerness to attend the shaykh's gatherings at a time when he was refusing to receive many French and Swiss journalists, should be sufficient to show you the extent of the Shaykh's influence on him and other orientalists."[71]

Guénon continued to live a Sufi life of retreat in Egypt but continued writing and publishing in specialist Western magazines published by various scholars to propagate those Eastern spiritual traditions they advocated as means of right guidance and spiritual advancement. Perhaps the most significant of these was the Swiss philosopher and artist, Frithjof Schuon. In 1932 he was sent by Guénon to Ahmad ibn Mustafa al-'Alawi, the shaykh of the 'Alawiyya Darqawiyya Shadhiliyya *tariqa* in Algeria, where he embraced Islam, taking the name 'Isa Nur ad-Deen Ahmad, and joined the Darqawiyya Shadhiliyya. In 1934, after the death of Shaykh al-'Alawi, Frithjof Schuon was appointed *muqaddim* of the 'Alawiyya Darqawiyya Shadhiliyya order in the West by the khalifa of Shaykh al-'Alawi, 'Adda Ben Tunis, evidenced by a document written in his own hand[72].

The supporters of Schuon consider this document to be an *ijaza* which both confirms Schuon's sincerity and also gives him the spiritual authority to found a branch of the 'Alawiyya Darqawiyya order in the West, which was to have unprecedented influence due to its complete independence from its base in Mostaganem in Algeria. He later changed its name to the Maryamiyya order. Others considered the contents of that document to be weak, deeming it to be merely a customary document, which did not in fact give Schuon any special authority to call people to himself or to anyone else, and that the call to Islam referred to in the document was general. Mark Sedgwick says in reference to it: "Indeed, all the things 'permitted' to Schuon in it are things for which no permission is needed, and which are actually incumbent upon any Muslim anyhow. The 'diplôme' thus has the form of an appointment without any substance. It is hard to think of any reason for Ibn Tunis to produce such an empty document, save perhaps to respond tactfully to a request for an *ijaza* with

---

71   Nassr Mutawalli Wahba, Faruq. *al-'Arif Billah: Sidi Salama ar-Radi: al-Faylasuf wa as-Sufi wa ash-Sha'ir wa al-Adib*, op. cit.

72   *See* Appendix, p.109

which he was unwilling to comply."[73]

The text of original document in the handwriting of the author appears:

3. THE WESTERN BRANCH OF THE ORDER:

A. Beginning of its foundation

After his return to Europe, Schuon established three *zawiyyas* – in Amiens, Paris, and Basel – all under the same name as that of the Mostaganem *zawiyya*: al-'Alawiyya ad-Darqawiyya. This gave Guénon a useful ally. Guénon, who was not a *muqaddim* and could not, therefore, initiate others, now had someone to whom he could send those Westerners who, having read his books and articles, had come to him for spiritual guidance. So Schuon, who was quite unknown at the time, found himself with a small but steady stream of followers. This means that it is really only from 1934 onwards that one can truly speak of a Western branch of the Darqawiyya Shadhiliyya (or more accurately, the 'Alawiyya Darqawiyya), inspired by a Frenchman, Guénon, and led by a Swiss German (Schuon) and made up entirely of Western *murids*.

Subsequently this branch would collect a number of people interested in the East, one of the most prominent of whom was Titus Burckhardt who had embraced Sufism in Morocco in 1930, following the path of one of the branches of the Darqawiyya. His written contributions include an important book entitled *Introduction to Sufi Doctrine*, as well as a translation of some of the letters of Moulay al-'Arabi ad-Darqawi. He also made many other contributions in the fields of art and Islamic civilisation through his regular propagation of traditional Sufi thought in the magazine, *Études Traditionnelles*.

All of this happened quietly without any overt publicity, because "the mid-1930s was not a good time to draw attention to oneself in many parts of Europe",[74] owing to the political and religious circumstances prevailing at the time. These included widespread prejudice against Islam, which covered all who defended it and, to an even greater extent, people who had actively embraced it, were influenced by its spirituality, and were

---

73 *See* Mark Sedgwick, "Traditionalist Sufism" op.cit., p5

74 Andrew Rawlinson, "A History of Western Sufism", Diskus, op. cit., pp. 45-83

1. Chapter Two: The Shadhili Sufi Tariqas in the West

trying to spread it in the West. Notwithstanding this, at the beginning of 1939 the Sufi circle of the Darqawiyya Shadhiliyya branch in the West comprised about a hundred members, moved intellectually by the books of Guénon and under the spiritual leadership of Frithjof Schuon.

"Things remained quiet during WWII, as might be expected. But in 1946, on the death of Sheikh Adda ben Tounis, head of the Alawiyya, Schuon was declared a sheikh by his Western disciples (and he only had Western disciples)."[75] Ignoring the issue of legitimacy of his own *bay'a*, and whether *murids* are able to elevate a person to the rank of shaykh without specific *idhn* from his shaykh, the elevation of Schuon to the position of shaykh had certain specific implications: "But the significance of Schuon's elevation to the level of sheikh was that he could now appoint *moqaddems* of his own (whereas before this time he had himself been a *muqaddim*). I know of two: Michel Valsan/Sheikh Mustafa,[76] a Roumanian serving in the diplomatic service in Paris and head of the Paris *khanqah*; and Martin Lings/Sheikh Abu Bakr Siraj ad-Din, who was Schuon's *muqaddim* in Britain. But relations between Guenon and Schuon became increasingly strained – partly because Schuon's disciples wanted to elevate Schuon to a higher position than Guénon (in fact, they wanted Guenon to be Schuon's *muqaddim* in Egypt); and partly because Guenon objected to what he saw as increasing eclecticism[77] in Schuon's teaching."[78]

Added to that was the gradual slide towards disassociation from the

---

75   Andrew Rawlinson "A History of Western Sufism", Diskus, op. cit., pp.45-83

76   Michel Valsan (1911–1974) was a Muslim scholar and master of the Shadhiliyya *tariqah* in Paris under the name of Shaykh Mustafa 'Abd al-'Aziz. He was also a Romanian diplomat and a prolific translator who specialised in translating and interpreting the works of the Sufi theoretician Ibn 'Arabi.

77   Eclecticism is a conceptual approach that does not hold rigidly to a single paradigm or set of assumptions, but instead draws upon multiple theories, styles, or ideas to gain complementary insights into a subject, or it applies different theories in particular cases. It can sometimes seem inelegant or lacking in simplicity, and eclectics are sometimes criticised for lack of consistency in their thinking. It is, however, common in many fields of study. For example, most psychologists accept certain aspects of behaviourism, but do not attempt to use the theory to explain all aspects of human behaviour. A statistician may use frequentist techniques on one occasion and Bayesian ones on another.

78   Andrew Rawlinson, "A History of Western Sufism", Diskus, op. cit., pp.45-83

Islamic Shari'a, which now began at the hands of Schuon. This included some practices, such as his allowing his followers not to fast in Ramadan and to drink wine in gatherings – which made others doubt their Islam – and other similar things, which he justified for them on the basis of the difficulty of living in an environment hostile to Islam. This was, however, a subject of scorn on the part of some of his followers, such as Michel Vâlsan, his *muqaddim* in Paris, and the subject of sharp criticism on the part of René Guénon.[79]

B. The beginning of the split: René Guénon and Frithof Schuon

By 1949, each of the two men, Guénon and Schuon, had gone their separate ways. Guenon remained a practising Muslim Sufi, following the Hamidiyya Shadhiliyya *tariqa*, living in retreat in Egypt and devoting himself to his writings, with the object of spreading traditionalist philosophy, of which he was the primary proponent and which subsequently even took his name when it became known as Guenonism. Schuon, on the other hand, continued with his branch of the Darqawiyya 'Alawiyya, which he distorted to a new form of Sufism whose esoteric spiritual teachings were derived from the Virgin Mary and became known as the Maryamiyya 'Alawiyya Darqawiyya order.[80]

Shaykh Mustafa (Michel Vâlsan)

The *muqaddim* of Schuon in Paris split from him at about the same time Schuon parted from Guénon, declaring himself and his group independent from Schuon's order. We do not know much about this group, except that it is certain that Valsan followed a purely Islamic path. He was known for his strictness in preserving Islamic practices, attending the Friday prayers in the mosque, carefully observing the prayers and the fast, performing the daily prayers on time along with the supererogatory prayers, and going to Makka twice, to fulfil the duty of hajj in 1965 and '*umra* in 1974.

---

79   Mark Sedgwick, *Against the Modern World: Traditionalism and the Secret Intellectual History of the Twentieth Century* op. cit., p.126

80   Mark Sedgwick, *Against the Modern World: Traditionalism and the Secret Intellectual History of the Twentieth Century,* op. cit., pp.147-160

1. Chapter Two: The Shadhili Sufi Tariqas in the West

He followed the strictest possible interpretation of the Shari'a, ensuring that his sons were taught the prayer from the age of seven. His son Muhammad fasted the month of Ramadan when he was five.[81]

The life of Michel Vâlsan resembled to some extent the Sufi saints of Allah. He was humble and abstemious with regard to this world, turning away from the many requests made to him to give lectures, wary of being attached to love of appearance. "His practice was entirely founded on the example of the Prophet Muhammad ﷺ and the works of Ibn 'Arabi."[82] After his death, his followers, who numbered about a hundred, split into a number of groups. At the end of the twentieth century, there were three groups who were active in different part of France. The shaykhs of these three groups attached themselves and their followers to regular Sufi orders in the Arab world: one of which was a branch of the 'Alawiyya in Damascus; the second was the most populous order which spread in its time in Syria and is a branch of the Naqshbandiyya which was led by the mufti of Damascus; and the third was connected to a branch of the Darqawiyya in North Africa.[83]

4. THE 'ALAWIYYA ORDER'S PIONEERS IN THE WEST

A. René Guénon

'Abdal-Halim Mahmud, the Shaykh of al-Azhar, said about René Guénon (on page 301 of his book *The Case of Sufism: the Shadhiliyya School*, published by the Dar al-Ma'arif al-Misriyya in Cairo in 1999): "Guénon was one of the personalities who have a place in history. Muslims compare him with Imam al-Ghazali and his like, and non-Muslims with Plotinus, the founder of Neo-Platonism, and his likes."

Michel Vâlsan, one of the great Western Sufis influenced by him, said, "The phenomenon of Guénon is one of the greatest intellectual marvels since the end of the Middle Ages in Europe." Muhammad Shurayh, the Palestinian scholar, says about him: "In the darkness of the twentieth

---

81   Mark Sedgwick, *Against the Modern World: Traditionalism and the Secret Intellectual History of the Twentieth Century*, op. cit., p.133

82   Ibid. p.135

83   Ibid. p.136

century, overshadowed by its materialism which is rushing humanity towards destruction at a rate unprecedented in the annals of speed calculation, in this century lost in the deserts of godlessness, in the nihilist existentialism of Sartre, in the dialectical materialism of Marx and in all the other barren modernisms of today's intellectual world, there appeared the phenomenon of Guénon. It was as if he truly was a marvel at the heart of modern civilisation; finally a living spirit had emerged from the world of men. This thin Frenchman lit a candle for the spirit in the heart of a Europe weighed down with the burdens of materialism and rekindled reflection on traditionalist culture – the culture of the spirit and saintliness – in a time of banality, lies and misguidance."[84]

In 'Abdal-Halim Mahmud's *The case of Sufism: the Shadhiliyya school*, we find on page 286 a statement from André Gide, quoting what he said after reading the works of Guénon: "If Guénon is right, well, all my oeuvre falls to the ground, and my entire life is shown to be without meaning." He added, "If I had read Guenon when I was young, I would have lived life another way."

Personality

The sources do not help us learn much about the early part of Rene Guénon's life. This is, according to the British thinker Martin Lings, because of his extreme reticence and his sense of objectivity and reluctance to talk about himself, which was, in fact, one aspect of his greatness.[85] It is known that the name on his birth certificate was Guénon, René-Jean-Marie-Joseph and it is dated 15 November 1886 in Blois in the Loire district in France. The name on his death certificate is 'Abd al-Wahid Yahya and it is dated 8 January 1951 in Cairo.

Guénon was distinguished from childhood by his keen intellect and poor health. He completed his studies in the city where he was born, obtaining the Baccalauréat in philosophy in 1904. He then went to Paris and, in 1906, enrolled in Rollin College with the object of gaining a degree in mathematics but, for a number of his reasons, he never

---

84 Muhammad Sharih, on: http://www.almultaka.net
85 Martin Lings, "René Guénon" in Sophia, Vol.1, No.1 (summer 1995) p.21

1. Chapter Two: The Shadhili Sufi Tariqas in the West

finished his studies. His academic life ends at this point and Jean-Claude Frère believes that it was the spiritual movements flooding Paris at that time which attracted him and probably diverted him from his original goal. Among them were theosophy and the various occult and esoteric movements of freemasonry, hermetic Martinism, different traditionalist knowledges and others as well.[86]

Guénon completely immersed himself in these esoteric movements and began to learn about one group after another and he was able to set up a network of personal connections with most of their leaders and representatives. However, he quickly grasped the fallacies they involved and began to attack them openly, refuting all the baseless, absurd and fanciful claims they were making. He later included these criticisms in some of his books, such as *Theosophy: history of a pseudo-religion* and *The Spiritist Fallacy*.

In 1912 Guénon embraced Islam and embarked on the path of Sufism at the hand of 'Abd al-Hadi 'Uqayli, which was the Muslim name of Ivan Gustaf Aguéli, and from that time on was usually known in the world of Shadhili Islamic Sufism by the name "'Abd al-Wahid Yahya." When the First World War started in 1914, Guénon turned to writing (since he was excused from the army for health reasons) but he also needed paid work in order to provide for his wife and niece and began to teach philosophy, firstly at different free foundations between 1916 and 1917, then in Setif, Algeria, at the end of 1917 and the first month of 1919, and finally, keeping a low profile, for a short time at the college of Blois. He was not, however, a success as a teacher and retired in 1919. Perhaps he was not suited for any worldly tasks!

Guénon's difficulties were exacerbated by the death of his French wife Berthe on 15 January 1928 who had, for 16 years, been a sincere and constant support to him in his studies and writing. Then nine months later, his aunt, who had stayed with him for a long time in his house in 51 rue Saint-Louis–en-île, also died. Finally, to complete his misery, the hand of fate took away his niece, who was only fourteen years old.[87] On

---

86 Khayyata, Nihad. "René Guénon wa al-Manqul al-haqiqi", Retrieved in August 10, 2007. from: http://maaber.50megs.com/issue_february06/spiritual_traditions2.htm#_ftn2

87 Khayyata, Nihad. "René Guénon wa al-Manqul al- haqiqi", op. cit.

5 March 1930 Guénon left France for Egypt where he remained until his death on 7 January 1951.

Throughout the whole of this period in Egypt Guénon, or Shaykh 'Abd al-Wahid as he was now known, lived a traditional Sufi Muslim life, spending most of his time in the mosque in *dhikr* and prayer and attending Sufi gatherings. However, at the same time, he was clearly anxious not to sever his links with Europe and it was during this period that he wrote in French his major works: *The Multiple States of Being*, *The Reign of Quantity & the Signs of the Times*, *The Symbolism of the Cross*, and *The Great Triad*. His earlier works: *East and West*, *The Crisis of the Modern World*, *The King of the World*, and *Spiritual Authority and Temporal Power* had already been published before he went to Egypt.

Despite the distance of Shaykh 'Abd al-Wahid Yahya from Europe and his rejection of fame in favour of the simple life he had chosen, the path forged by his intellect brought him fervent followers from among the cream of the educated European élite. The best known of his followers and students were probably Michel Vâlsan, Frithjof Schuon, Titus Burckhardt, Marco Pallis, René Allar, and André Préau, among others.

The influence of Guénon continued to grow in the academic world. He and his writings had a clear effect on important figures in the academic domain. We can mention among them Mircea Eliade and Henry Corbin. And in the field of literature, André Gide and André Breton are perhaps the most famous writers to have been affected by Guénon's life and writings.[88] In all he wrote about twenty-nine books and five hundred essays on the subject of traditionalism, faith, vision and criticism of the modern world.

His Books

Guénon became one of the most famous faces of Islam to participate actively in bringing together the East and the West but most of his works are still unknown in the Western world since only a few were translated from French into other languages. His books include:

1. *East and West*
2. *The Crisis of the Modern World*

[88] Muhammad Sharih, on: http://www.almultaka.net

1. Chapter Two: The Shadhili Sufi Tariqas in the West

3. *The Esotericism of Dante*
4. *The Great Triad*
5. *Initiation and Spiritual Realization*
6. *Insights into Christian Esoterism*
7. *Insights into Islamic Esoterism and Taoism*
8. *Introduction to the Study of the Hindu Doctrines*
9. *The King of the World*
10. *Man and His Becoming According to the Vedanta*
11. *The Multiple States of Being*
12. *Perspectives on Initiation*
13. *The Spiritist Fallacy*
14. *Spiritual Authority and Temporal Power*
15. *Studies in Hinduism*
16. *The Symbolism of the Cross*
17. *Symbols of Sacred Science*
18. *Traditional Forms and Cosmic Cycles*

B. Frithjof Schuon

His Life

Frithjof Schuon was born in the city of Basel in Switzerland in 1907 to German parents. While still a child he went to Paris where he studied for a number of years before undertaking a number of journeys to North Africa, the Near East and India, in order to witness at first hand traditionalist cultures and to make a direct connection with spiritual sources. Frithjof Schuon was also known in the Muslim world by the name of Shaykh 'Isa Nur ad-Deen Ahmad ash-Shadhili ad-Darqawi al-'Alawi al-Maryami. He was one of the main proponents of Traditional Metaphysics and Philosophia Perennis.

Due to his French education, Frithjof Schuon wrote most of his books in the language of Victor Hugo and they did not begin to be translated until the appearance in English of his first book, *The Transcendent Unity of Religions*, in 1953, about which the English poet, T.S. Eliot, said, "I have met with no more impressive work in the comparative study of Oriental and Occidental religion."[89]

Schuon was a metaphysical Sufi and most of his books were about traditionalist subjects and principles which he was the first to apply in Sufi practice. He was also a poet and artist. He has a very large collection of published works which include two long lyrical poems and more than a hundred poems in English. In his art he inclined to simplicity of style, drawing objects and people in such a way as to reflect the natural form and origin of man. Perhaps the most notable of his drawings, and the most contentious, are his depiction of the Virgin Mary naked as she is supposed to have appeared to him a vision. This became a symbol of what he called "holy nakedness" and was turned into one of the most important rites of his order after it became the Maryamiyya.

As a young man in Paris, Schuon became interested in Islam, and he embarked on a rigorous study of Arabic, visiting North Africa a number of times. In 1930 he became a *murid* of the Sufi Shaykh Ahmad ibn Mustafa al-'Alawi. In 1949 he married in Lausanne, Switzerland, and he and his wife were given a plot of land with an orchard and vineyard in Pully, a suburb east of the city, where they built their home. In 1950 Schuon had contact for the first time with North American Indians and he and his wife were adopted into the Red Cloud family of the Lakota tribe of the Sioux nation in 1959, and also by the Crow tribe. In his last years he lived in Indiana and died there from a protracted illness in 1998.

All of Schuon's work reaffirms traditional metaphysical principles, interpreting the esoteric dimensions of religion, penetrating mythological and religious forms, and critiquing modernism. He clarified the distinctions between the exoteric and esoteric dimensions of religious tradition and attempted to reveal the metaphysical convergence of all orthodox religions.[90] In a number of his books, he prefers Islam to other religions. In this context we can mention his book, *Iman, Islam and Ihsan compared with other religions,* in which he extols the strength of Islam compared with some other religions: "Islam, with its distinguishing form

---

89   Frithjof Schuon, *The Transcendent Unity of Religions*, Translated by: Peter Townsend, Harper & Row (1975).

90   Sophia, Journal of Traditional Studies, vol. 4, no. 2, Winter 1998, (which is dedicated to the memory of Frithjof Schuon).

1. Chapter Two: The Shadhili Sufi Tariqas in the West

and spiritual means, has a simple structure, which can repair any specific ruptures occurring in older and more ancient religions and combat the seeds of corruption stemming from such ruptures."[91]

There is also his book *Understanding Islam* in which he attempts to present a metaphysical picture of Islam, the Noble Qur'an and the Sunna of the Prophet ﷺ and also of the Prophet ﷺ himself and the Sufi path.[92] His third book about Islam entitled *Islam and the Perennial Philosophy* is an attempt to study Islamic principles and ideas and compare them with other religions with the aim of extrapolating the unity of these religions on an inner level despite the necessity of differences at an outward level.[93]

His books[94]

He has a very large collection of works and books. Seyyed Hossein Nasr, one of the prominent academic experts on him now in the West, says about him:

> "His works which he wrote in French have been translated into most European languages and have now also been translated into most Islamic languages, such as Arabic, Persian, Malaysian and Urdu; indeed, one of his books was originally published in India. His thoughts are known, not only on both sides of the Atlantic Ocean, but also throughout the entire world from Malaysia to Morocco and from South Africa to Brazil."[95]

---

91 Frithjof Schuoun, *al-Iman al-Islam wa al-Ihsan fi Muqaranati al-Adyan*, translated by: Nihad Khayyata, Univesity press for Studies, Print and Publication: Beirut. 1st edition (1996CE/1416AH). p.15

92 Frithjof Schuon, *Comprendre l'Islam*, Editions du Seuil (1976), Imprimerie Hérissey à Evreaux.

93 Frithjof Schuon, *Islam and the Perennial Philosophy*, Translated by: J. Peter Hobson, Preface by: Seyyed Hossein Nasr, World of Islam Festival Company Ltd., 1976.

94 Ibid. p.28

95 Seyyed Hossein Nasr, "The Biography of Frithjof Schuon", in *Religion of the Heart (essays presented to Frithjof Schuon on his eightieth birthday)*, edited by: Seyyed Hossein Nasr & William Stoddart, Foundation For Traditional Studies, Washington,D.C. (1991), p.1.

Despite the exaggeration and adulation contained in this statement, the man was in truth an innovator who wrote a lot of books which deal with Sufism, wisdom and gnosis. They are listed here according to when they were first published:

1. *The Transcendent Unity of Religions* (1953)
2. *Stations of Wisdom* (1961)
3. *Logic and Transcendence* (1975)
4. *Esotericism as Principle and as Way* (1981)
5. *From the Divine to the Human* (1982)
6. *Light on the Ancient Worlds* (1984)
7. *Christianity/Islam: Essays on Esoteric Ecumenicism* (1985)
8. *Survey of Metaphysics and Esotericism* (1986)
9. *Spiritual Perspective and Human Facts* (1987)
10. *In the Face of the Absolute* (1989)
11. *The Feathered Sun* (1990)
12. *Gnosis: Divine Wisdom* (1990)
13. *To have a Center* (1990)
14. *Echoes of Perennial Wisdom* (1992)
15. *Understanding Islam* (1994)

C. Martin Lings

The Phenomenon

Shaykh Ahmad al-Qar'ani said, "Despite his lack of recognition among the Sufis of the Arab lands, Hajj Abu Bakr Siraj ad-Deen (Martin Lings) is considered to be among the most significant contemporary men of Sufism, and his Sufi views and statements are regarded with respect and interest. It is enough to know that fewer than a dozen specialists among his contemporaries have been selected to write articles on Sufism in the last publication of the British Da'ira al-Ma'arif." [96]

The Syrian writer Muhammad 'Isam 'Adu says about him with respect to his standing: "Martin Lings (Abu Bakr Siraj ad-Deen) is considered one of the most important writers, or rather important Western academics,

---

96 Ahmad al-Kat'ani, *Hurras al-'aqida*, Library of Méknes for Print and Publication. Tripoli: Libya. 2nd edition (2001 CE/1422AH). p.105

1. Chapter Two: The Shadhili Sufi Tariqas in the West

to have presented to the West a profound recognition of its inheritance from Islam and its gnostic tradition." The fame of this Islamic scholar, or master of spirituality, is such that, in the words of Shusha Guppy in The Independent, "at a time when so much nonsense is talked about 'clashes of civilisations' and Islam is under siege, the work of Martin Lings shines like a beacon."

He is the author of the most famous contemporary biography of the Prophet, *Muhammad: His Life Based on the Earliest Sources*, a book whose reading is considered indispensable for every Westerner when they want to learn something about Islam.

He is part of one of the most important circles of the Illuminationist school or "Perennial Philosophy" in Britain, since he was considered to be one of the most important thinkers of this perennialist school after his Swiss teacher Frithjof Schuon or 'Isa Nur ad-Deen.[97]

Fuad Nahdi, the owner of Q-News, the leading Islamic magazine in Britain, says about him: "For indeed Shaykh Abu Bakr is a mountain among the molehills of our times: a peak so glorious and beautiful that it can only provoke awe for those who are at its feet and breathlessness for those who want to even contemplate making an effort to genuinely reach it."[98]

The American Muslim proselytizer Mark Hanson, or Hamza Yusuf, describes him by saying: "Martin Lings was a spiritual giant in an age of dwarfed terrestrial aspirations and endeavors."[99]

His life

Martin Lings was born in Manchester in the north of England on 24th January 1909. He spent his childhood in the U.S. with his father before returning to go to school at Clifton College, Bristol. Then he went to Magdalen College, Oxford, where his poetical gifts first appeared. He

---

[97] Muhammad 'Issam 'Idu, "Intafa Siraju Abu Bakr – Martin Lings" (2005CE/1909AH), Retrieved from the cultural forum: http://www.almultaka.net/makalat.php?subaction=showfull&id=1117481536&archive=&start_from=&ucat=3&

[98] Fuad Nahdi, "Q-News", June (2005), n:363, p:47

[99] Hamza Yusuf, "Q-News", June (2005), n:363, p:53

got his B.A. degree in English literature in 1932 and his M.A. in the same subject in 1937. While at Oxford, he also began a friendship with C.S. Lewis, his tutor, that would last for the remainder of Lewis' life and was destined to have a great effect on the course of Lings's thought.

After teaching English in Poland, Lings was appointed lecturer at the University of Kaunas in Lithuania, where he remained until 1939. After that he went to Cairo where, from 1940 to 1951, he taught English language and literature – primarily Shakespeare – at Cairo university. Every year he also staged a number of Shakespeare's plays. Having left Egypt for political reasons, he joined the British Library in 1955 to work as Keeper of Arabic Manuscripts, eventually becoming the Keeper of Oriental Manuscripts at the British Museum until his retirement in 1972. His work in the British Museum and Library led to him publishing a book about Arabic Calligraphy, *The Qur'anic Art of Calligraphy and Illumination*.

Lings obtained his doctorate from the University of London in 1959. It was about Shaykh Ahmad ibn Mustafa al-'Alawi and was published under the title *A Sufi saint of the Twentieth Century: Shaikh Ahmad al-'Alawi, his spiritual heritage and legacy*. That book can be considered as a synopsis of the life-path of Martin Lings, and the results of his journey in Sufism and spiritual reflection burst forth from it. A sincere search for the truth was in general one of the hallmarks of his life and led him to the discovery of the books of René Guénon, whose intellectual insights helped him to grasp the fallacies of the contemporary world in which religion had become sidelined. His awareness was awakened to the fact that inner truth is not confined to a single religious tradition but is common to all divine religions. He says about the books of Guénon, "I knew that I was face to face with the Truth. It was almost like being struck by lightning... I knew that something must be done about this."[100] That is how it came about that Lings chose to convert to Islam, since the Islamic religion, being the last, is by that fact superior to other religious forms because of its nearness in time, something which is reflected in the freshness, vibrancy and dynamism of the teachings of its spiritual core, Sufism.

---

100 Michael Fitzgerald, "In Memoriam: Dr. Martin Lings" in: "Vincit Omnia Veritas" II, 1, p.90

1. Chapter Two: The Shadhili Sufi Tariqas in the West

Another impetus for his conversion was the request of his shaykh, Frithjof Schuon, who wrote to him in a letter: "If you want to join us, you must embrace Islam,"[101] which he did at the hand of Titus Burckhardt, the representative of Schuon in Basel.[102] Schuon was, at that time, acting as *muqaddim* of the 'Alawiyya Darqawiyya Shadhiliyya order in the West and Lings became one of its most important figures in the West and a muqaddim of the *tariqa* in Britain before he went along with Schuon in changing its name to the Maryamiyya 'Alawiyya order. However, he continued on Islamic lines until his death on 12 May 2005, only a few days after celebrating the Mawlud of the Messenger Muhammad ﷺ at the Conference Centre in the city of Wembley in Britain on 2 May 2005.

Throughout his life, Lings remained sincere to Islamic Sufi principles. Despite his belief in the universality of Sufism, he also believed in the necessity of practising it within an Islamic structure. He says in the second section of his book, *What is Sufism?*: "Those who insist that Sufism is 'free of the shackles of religion' do so partly because they imagine that its universality is at stake. But however sympathetic we may feel towards their preoccupation with this undoubted aspect of Sufism, it must not be forgotten that particularity is perfectly compatible with universality, and in order to perceive this truth in an instant we have only to consider… Islamic art."[103]

His books

Martin Lings produced a large collection of literary, Sufic and intellectual works which are in the form of essays and books. Some of his most important published books in various languages, but mainly English, are:

1. *Splendours of Qur'an Calligraphy and Illumination* (2005)
2. A *Return to the Spirit: Questions and Answers* (2005)
3. *Sufi Poems: A Mediaeval Anthology* (2005)

101 "Sophia" Vol.4 (1998), No.2, op. cit., 16-17

102 Ibid. p.16-17

103 Martin Lings, *What Is Sufism?*, The Islamic Texts Society (1993), Cambridge, UK, p.17

4. *Mecca: From Before Genesis until Now* (2004)
5. *The Eleventh Hour: the Spiritual Crisis of the Modern World in the Light of Tradition and Prophecy* (2006)
6. *Collected Poems, revised and expanded* (2002)
7. *Ancient Beliefs and Modern Superstitions* (2001)
8. *The Secret of Shakespeare*
9. *Sacred Art of Shakespeare*
10. *A Sufi Saint of the Twentieth Century*
11. *Symbol and Archetype*
12. *Muhammad: His Life Based on the Earliest Sources* (1983)
13. *The Quran'ic Art of Calligraphy and Illumination* (1976)
14. *What is Sufism?* (1975)
15. *The Book of Certainty*

Some people consider Ling's books, *Muhammad: His Life Based on the Earliest Sources*, *A Sufi Saint of the Twentieth Century: Shaikh Ahmad al-'Alawi, His Spiritual Heritage and Legacy* and *What is Sufism?*, which have a distinctive, poetic style, to be the best written in English about Islam and Islamic Sufism.

D. Titus Burckhardt

His Life

He was a Swiss Sufi thinker who was born in Florence in 1908 and died in Lausanne in 1984. He devoted most of his life to the study and exposition of the different aspects of Traditional Wisdom. In the age of modern science and technology, Titus Burckhardt was one of the most remarkable exponents of Universal Truth, both in the realm of metaphysics and also in the realm of cosmology and of traditional art. In a world of existentialism, psychoanalysis, and sociology, he was a major voice of the philosophia perennis that is expressed in Platonism, Vedanta, Sufism, Taoism, and other authentic esoteric or traditional teachings. In his literary and philosophical output he showed himself to be an eminent member of the "traditionalist" or "perennialist" school of 20th century thinkers and writers headed by the French Muslim Sufi, René Guénon.

Burckhardt, in the wake of his immediate forebears, was very aware of art, architecture and Islamic civilisation, and he also wrote, published

1. Chapter Two: The Shadhili Sufi Tariqas in the West

and translated books about Islamic Sufism such as The Letters of Shaykh al-'Arabi ad-Darqawi (1760-1823) and some of the works of Muhyi ad-Deen ibn 'Arabi (1165-1240) and 'Abd al-Karim al-Jili (1365 -1424).

Although Titus Burckhardt was born in Florence, his family were Swiss from Basel. His grandfather was the famous art historian Jacob Burckhardt and his father was the sculptor, Carl Burckhardt. He was a contemporary of Frithjof Schuon and, along with him, was one of the leaders of traditionalist thought. They spent their early days together in Basel at around the time of the First World War and this was the beginning of an intimate friendship and a deeply harmonious intellectual and spiritual relationship that was to last a lifetime.[104] Burckhardt was the representative (or *muqaddim*) of the 'Alawiyya Darqawiyya Shadhiliyya group of Sufis in Basel, Switzerland.

His books

He wrote a number of books in German, French and English, mostly on Sufism, wisdom, and sacred art. The most important are:

1. *The Letters of a Sufi Master: Shaykh al-'Arabi ad-Darqawi*
2. *Fes, City of Islam* 1992
3. *An Introduction to Sufi Doctrine*
4. *Moorish Culture in Spain* 1999
5. *Art of Islam: Language and Meaning*
6. *Siena, City of the Virgin* 1960
7. *Famous Illuminated Manuscripts*, 1964
8. *Mirror of the Intellect: Essays of Traditional Science and Sacred Art*, 1987.
9. *The Universality of Sacred Art*, 1999
10. *Sacred Art in the East and West*, 1967
11. *Alchemy, Science of the Cosmos, Science of the Soul*, 1967
12. *Mystical Astrology according to Ibn 'Arabi*, 1977
13. *The Foundations of Christian Art* 2006

---

104 William Stoddart, "Titus Burckhardt and the Perennialist School" in: http://religioperennis.org/documents/stoddart/TB.pdf viewed: 15/08/2007

TOPIC TWO
OTHER SHADHILI ORDERS

Whatever sharp criticism can be directed to the Western branch of the 'Alawiyya Darqawiyya Shadhiliyya order, it is not possible to overlook one of the most important of its beauties. It opened the way, either through writing or practice, for many Westerners to discover this abundant spring of overflowing spirituality in the religion of Islam. There have been many academic studies in different Western universities about this phenomenon and seekers of inner truth travelled to the East to take Sufism from its original shaykhs. Because of this new Sufi groups began to appear in the West whose teachings were derived from the spiritual core of Islam and who were able to adapt them to the Western environment. A beautiful mosaic was formed made up of different groups dominated by the Shadhili *tariqa*.

1. THE HASHIMIYYA DARQAWIYYA SHADHILIYYA ORDER

A. Foreword

This is one of the most prominent of the Darqawi Shadhili branches in the West, especially in the U.S.A. It is distinct from the Western branch of the Shahdiliyya we have just been looking at because of the fact that it views Sufism as a purely Islamic phenomenon. They see Sufism as something inseparable from the Islamic Shari'a which is the only vessel able to contain its spiritual reality. Its present shaykh in both the West and in the Arab world is Nuh Ha Mim Keller.

B. The Life of its Shaykh

Shaykh Nuh Keller was born in 1954 in the farming country of the north-western United States to a Roman Catholic family. He says about himself when recounting the story of his path to Islam: "I was raised in a religious family as a Roman Catholic. The Church provided a spiritual world that was unquestionable in my childhood, if anything more real than the physical world around me, but as I grew older, and especially after I entered a Catholic university and read more, my relation to the

1. Chapter Two: The Shadhili Sufi Tariqas in the West

religion became increasingly called into question, in belief and practice. Moreover, when I went to the university, I found that the authenticity of the book, especially the New Testament, had come into considerable doubt as a result of modern hermeneutical studies by Christians themselves."[105]

Bit by bit the philosophical problems became greater in his mind until Nuh Keller found himself inclining to Islam. He says: "Christianity had its good points to be sure, but they seemed mixed with confusions, and I found myself more and more inclined to look to Islam for their fullest and most perfect expression."[106] That is why Keller embraced Islam in 1977 in Cairo where he was studying Arabic and Islamic Studies at al-Azhar University, specialising in hadith and the fundamentals of *fiqh*. He obtained high degrees and *ijazas* from al-Azhar University and from a number of Syrian and Jordanian shaykhs, who gave him permission to transmit knowledge in *fiqh* and *'aqida*.[107]

In 1980 he moved to 'Amman, Jordan where he continues to live to this day. Keller took Islamic Sufism directly from its Shadhili source in his shaykh 'Abd ar-Rahman ash-Shaghouri, the author of the Diwan, *The Dewy Gardens in the Spiritual Breezes*. Shaykh ash-Shaghouri was born in Homs in 1912 to a Husayni family. He went to Damascus in 1922 where he studied Islamic sciences and received Shadhili authority in Sufi teaching from its shaykhs: Muhammad Hashimi, Sa'id al-Kurdi and others. He acknowledged himself as the heir of the secret of the "Hashimi Darqawi Shadhili path." His companions held *hadras* in an-Nuriyya Mosque in Damascus.[108] Some studies indicate that Shaykh 'Abd ar-Rahman ash-Shaghouri took Shadhili Sufism by two paths:

105 Nuh Ha Mim Keller, "Becoming Muslim" in: http://www.masud.co.uk/ISLAM/nuh/bmuslim.htm, viewed: 10/08/2007

106 Ibid.

107 Fatima Harrak, "Le Soufisme Face A La Mondialisation: Cas Des Confréries D'Origine Africaine Aux USA" dans: Confréries Soufis d'Afrique: Nouveaux Rôles: Nouveaux Enjeux, 2004, Actes du Colloque International, Organise par l'Institut des Etudes Africaines Rabat, 2-4 Octobre 2001, p.194

108 Marcia Hermansen, "The 'Other' Shadhilis of the West" in *The Shadhiliyya*, op. cit., p.495

1. From Shaykh Muhammad Saʻid al-Kurdi who was born in Jordan in 1892 and studied traditional Islamic sciences in Damascus. He lived in a small centre close to the city of Irbid where he died in 1972 at the age of 82. Shaykh al-Kurdi was a pure Sufi, Ashʻari in creed and Shafi'i in *madhhab*, who held to the Sunna and obliged his people to do the same.

2. Shaykh Hashimi (d. 1961), who was the student of Shaykh Ahmad Mustafa al-ʻAlawi, the Shaykh of the ʻAlawiyya Darqawiyya Shadhiliyya order in Mostaghanem, Algeria.

Ha Mim Keller is considered to be a model of the first generation of Western Sufis who studied Arabic and Islamic sources extensively. He now has a wide network of followers in the West, particularly the U.S.A., as well as in the Middle East, and many of his followers in the West consist of well-educated children of emigrant Muslims as well as Westerners who have converted to Islam.

C. His Sufic teachings

They do not differ in any way from the teachings of the Sufi orders in the Islamic world. They do not look at Sufism from a universalist perspective, as Inayat Khan did, nor from a traditionalist or perennial perspective, as Guénon and Schuon did. Rather Sufism is considered by him to be "the reality of *ihsan*" which can only be grasped by clinging to and being confined within the parameters of the Islamic Shariʻa. This makes some supporters of the universalist or traditionalist perspective describe the Sufic teachings which Keller transmits to his *murids* as "ultra orthodoxy" or "techno-*fiqh*". Others, however, consider it to be, Islamically speaking, the most authentic method, because it is based on adherence to traditional Sufism and the Islamic Shariʻa.[109]

The *tariqa* of Keller in the west is now in constant growth and will probably become even more significant in the near future since reports indicate that thousands of people attend his lectures in Europe, Canada and the U.S.A.[110]

---

[109] Marcia Hermansen, "The 'Other' Shadhilis of the West" in *The Shadhiliyya*, op. cit., p.495

[110] Marcia Hermansen, "The 'Other' Shadhilis of the West" in *The Shadhiliyya*, op. cit., p.496

1. Chapter Two: The Shadhili Sufi Tariqas in the West

D. His works and writings

One of the most significant projects undertaken by Nuh Ha Mim Keller is the translation of a number of texts of *fiqh* and *'aqida* into English. One of these is the legal work of Ahmad ibn an-Naqib al-Misri: *'Umdat as-Salik wa 'uddat an-Nasik*, which is the first legal work to appear in a European language and obtain a certificate of accuracy from al-Azhar.[111] There is also *al-Maqasid* by an-Nawawi as well as other texts. He also has a number of articles which can be accessed electronically in English. They include:

– Kalam and Islam
– Becoming Muslim (in which he tells the story of how he became Muslim)
– The Adab of Islam
– The Adab of the Sunna
– The Fiqh of Sunna
– The Woman: a parable commenting on the tragic events of September 11th 2001.

But his recent production of a splendid edition of the *Dala'il al-Khayrat* by the Moroccan Sufi Imam Muhammad ibn Sulayman al-Jazuli is one which has earned him much praise on the part of Sufis everywhere and that of others who are interested in such works.[112]

2. THE BATTAWIYYA SHADHILIYYA ORDER

A. The life of its Shaykh and his teachings

This small branch of the Shadhiliyya in the West is represented by Shaykh 'Abdullah Nooruddeen Durkee who is considered to be one of the leaders of Islamic Sufism in the U.S.A. He embraced Islam in 1974. After meeting the Palestinian Shahdili Shaykh Muhammad Jamal in the middle of the seventies, Shaykh Durkee and a group of his followers founded an Islamic settlement in New Mexico called Dar al-Islam which, in 1979, was the only American Islamic foundation. Later he returned to the Middle East where he lived for a long time in Alexandria, Egypt, in the

---

111 http://www.masud.co.uk/ISLAM/nuh/default.htm, viewed: 10/08/2007
112 http://www.dalail.co.uk/home.htm

company of his teacher in Shari'a sciences and his shaykh in Shadhiliyya Sufism, Ibrahim al-Battawi,[113] only returning to the U.S.A. in 1994.

Currently 'Abdullah Nooruddeen Durkee is the khalifa of Shaykh Ibrahim Muhammad al-Battawi in North America in particular and the West in general. He now lives in Virginia and is considered to be one of the most prominent activists calling people to Islam inside American prisons. He is also considered to be a fine speaker, moving between five local mosques, within a radius of about fifty miles, to give the Friday *khutba*. That is why he calls himself the "travelling shaykh".[114]

Shaykh Durkee is respected by all the shaykhs of Sufism in the West, especially in the U.S.A., as he has good relations with all Islamic groups of other Sufis there. His teachings do not differ much from the teachings of Nuh Ha Mim Keller since they are based on the connection between Sufism and the Islamic Shari'a in both theory and practice and he relies in his teachings on living Sufism by taking an active social role, doing things like caring for orphans, assisting the sick and prisoners. He shares in this activity with his wife, Hajja Nura Durkee. In the area of Sufic teaching, giving *dhikrs* and renewing *wirds*, he restricts himself to the teachings of his eastern shaykh Ibrahim Muhammad al-Battawi as his khalifa in the West.

B. His books

— *The Book of Exile,* a part of which has been published as *Embracing Islam*, which recounts the story of his coming to Islam.

— A book on the *tajwid* of the Noble Qur'an with all its suras, which has an online version for teaching the *tajwid* of the Qur'an.[115]

— A translation of the book *The Shadhili School* into English.

He is currently busy translating the Shadhili Sufi books of 'Abd al-Halim Mahmud and 'Abd al-Wafa at-Taftazani.[116]

He has a large collection of essays in English about divine love, Sufism,

---

113 He is the spiritual guide of the Shadhiliya Battawiya Sufi Tariqa.

114 Marcia Hermansen, "The 'Other' Shadhilis of the West" in *The Shadhiliyya*, op. cit., p.492

115 http://itajweed.org/testing/main.html viewed 10/08/2007

116 Marcia Hermansen, "The 'Other' Shadhilis of the West" in *The Shadhiliyya*, op. cit., p.492

1. Chapter Two: The Shadhili Sufi Tariqas in the West

recitation of the Qur'an as a spiritual practice, Muslim-Christian Dialogue and Jewish-Muslim Encounters.[117]

3. THE HABIBIYYA DARQAWIYYA SHADHILIYYA ORDER

There is also another order which travels the same path as that of the Battawiyya order and Hashimi Darqawi order in that it makes no split between Sufism and the Shari'a, even if it differs from them in its political views and religious impetus. It is the Habibiyya Darqawiyya order of its Scottish shaykh Ian Dallas.

A. General view

The Habibiyya Daqawiyya order is named after the Moroccan Sufi, Muhammad ibn al-Habib ad-Darqawi. It is currently overseen in the West by the Scottish Shaykh, Ian Dallas, who embraced Islam in the mid-1960s in the Karaouine Mosque in Fez. He was given the title 'as-Sufi' by Shaykh Muhammad ibn al-Habib with whom he stayed until his death in 1972. In 1978 Ian Dallas announced himself shaykh of this order in the West, disseminating the *tariqa* widely in Europe and the U.S. among new converts to Islam and the new generation of the children of Muslim emigrants.

The Habibiyya order turned into the Worldwide Murabitun Movement at the beginning of the 1980s, with the specific aim of re-establishing Islam in a comprehensive way and with particular emphasis on reviving the pillar of zakat, which the Muslims have lost, and on rediscovering the correct Islamic financial and economic landscape that this entails.

B. The teachings of the Habibiyya order

Shaykh Ian Dallas bases his teachings on full adherence to three principles which are considered to be central to building the complete Islamic personality and balanced sound Islamic society. They are:
- Holding to the Maliki school in Islamic *fiqh*
- Holding to the Ash'arite creed, which is agreed upon by the

---

117 http://www.greenmountainschool.org/essays.htm viewed:10/08/2007

people of the Sunna and the community
- Holding to a balanced legal Sufism with no ecstatic utterances or philosophy, an active Sufism which participates in founding a society economically, intellectually and politically

In the second section of this book we will deal in detail with the teachings of this order and life of its shaykh, his works and books, and the Moroccan Sufi influence behind it.

Section Two

The Moroccan Influence in Britain: Through the Model of the Habibiyya Darqawiyya Order

CHAPTER ONE

THE HABIBIYYA DARQAWIYYA ORDER

FOREWORD

Britain had no direct contact with Morocco during the colonial period and so was not a preferred destination for Moroccan immigrants but, despite that, we find the Moroccan brand of Islam has a very considerable presence in that country, a presence which Moroccan Sufism has greatly embellished, both by means of literature and practice. After studying this phenomenon from various angles I have ascertained that the Moroccan Sufi presence in Britain can be divided into four categories:

1. The presence in Britain of actual branches of Moroccan orders
2. The presence of British shaykhs who became Muslims and Sufis in Morocco and have spread Moroccan Sufism in the West, starting in Britain
3. A presence due to Moroccan Sufi texts which have been translated into English
4. A presence brought about by academic studies and research into Moroccan Sufism which has been carried out in Britain

The study of each of these four categories requires its own independent research if the presence of so many Moroccan Sufi orders in Britain is to be properly understood, but because of the diversity of studies and books which have looked at the subject of Moroccan Sufism, and the varied lines of investigation they have taken at different times, I have undertaken to study one order which in a way combines all these four categories. This is the Moroccan Habibiyya Darqawiyya order which has a presence in Britain due to the Scottish shaykh Ian Dallas.

Although this presence is the object of my study, the great role played in Britain by other Moroccan orders there such as, for example, the Budshishiyya order, should not be ignored. The Budshishiyya have established an active presence in Britain, propagating Islam from a Sufic perspective. Its influence in a number of British cities such as Birmingham,[118] the capital London,[119] Bradford[120] and Nottingham,[121] is clear evidence of this. These have all been established on the authority of the mother *zawiya* in Madagh, close to Berkane in eastern Morocco, which organises meetings and conferences to propagate Islam in general and Sufism in particular.

The order holds meetings for *dhikr* which are attended by both Muslim immigrants to Britain and also by many English people who have become Muslim or desire to embrace Islam. These gatherings for *dhikr* are a direct reflection of pure Moroccan Sufism. They begin with the recitation of some verses of the Noble Qur'an in the Warsh reading which prevails in Morocco and these are followed immediately by the Budshishiyya *wazifa*, a collection of *dhikrs* and prayers on the Messenger of Allah ﷺ which the Moroccan Shaykh of the Budshishiyya has enjoined on all his followers everywhere. After this there are some instructional words accompanied by glasses of Moroccan tea, following which there is Sufi *sama'* conducted in the Moroccan style and finally a meal which is eaten in the Moroccan way.[122]

The Budshishiyya order is considered by Anglo-Saxon scholars to be extremely important and, in the opinion of the American scholar Mark Sedgwick, it represents a unique Islamic phenomenon, since it has been able, in his view, to lead a counter reformation of Sufism, which was in

118   http://www.sufiway.net/zawiya_birmingham.html
119   http://www.sufiway.net/zawiya_london.html
120   http://www.sufiway.net/zawiyabradford.html
121   http://www.sufiway.net/znottingham.html
122   http://www.sufiway.net/zawiya_london.html

danger of disappearing at the end of the nineteenth and beginning of the twentieth century due to the negative political effects of reformist Islamic movements, such as the Salafiyya, that were hostile to Sufism.[123]

However, returning to the subject which was the starting point for this research paper, namely the new phenomenon of Sufi orders in the West led by Westerners, or what may be called, "Western Sufism", this chapter will be entirely dedicated to the study of the Habibiyya Darqawiyya order in the West and the extent to which Moroccan influence can be observed within it.

This study intends to answer the following questions. What are the roots of the Habibiyya order? Who is its current *murshid*? What are the distinguishing marks and special characteristics of its teachings? What is the true purpose behind the frequent criticisms made against it in the West and in the Muslim World? How does the Moroccan presence manifest itself in its Sufic teachings? There are many other questions and ambiguities about this order which ongoing studies are trying to deal with fully with the assistance of existing sources.

TOPIC ONE
THE MOROCCAN HABIBIYYA DARQAWIYYA ORDER

1. GENERAL FOREWORD

The Habibiyya Darqawiyya order was founded by the Moroccan Shaykh Muhammad ibn al-Habib, who was al-Idrisi al-Hasani by lineage and ad-Darqawi by ascription. He took Sufism from the al-Badawi ad-Darqawi ash-Shahdhli line and became the Qutb of his time in Sufism, able to renew the Darqawi way. As 'Abdalqadir as-Sufi says in his preface to the translation of the Diwan of Ibn al-Habib:

> "Within his lifetime there were deep changes within the discipline of the Tariq also. When he had taken the *wird* as a young man from the desert Shaykh, Sidi al-'Arabi al-Huwari, the Darqawa *fuqara'* were held to strict and difficult obligations. They wore the

---

[123] Mark Sedgwick "In Search of the Counter-Reformation: Anti-Sufi Stereotypes and the Budshishiyya's Response" in: Charles Kurzman and Michael Browers, eds., *An Islamic Reformation?* Lanham, Md: Lexington Books, 2004

muraqqa', the patched robe or *jellaba* and that only as far as just below the knees. Their *tasbih* beads were large and heavy wooden balls, so that the whole *tasbih* hung below the waist. Many went barefoot and carried the staff, some, even, the begging bowl. Under Shaykh Muhammad ibn 'Ali of Marrakesh the *fuqara'* were permitted to wear the *muraqqa'* longer in the bitter winters of the desert. They still recited the two hour long *wird* of Shaykh Muhammad al-'Arabi, the Master who followed the great khalif of Shaykh ad-Darqawi, Shaykh al-Badawi. When the permission came to Shaykh ibn al-Habib, he changed everything. Breaking with the tradition as the traditional culture which supported these things itself broke up, he issued new obligations. Instead of the *muraqqa'*, he ordered his *fuqara'* to wear the best clothes their station in life permitted. He rescinded the long *wird* and replaced it with his own *wird*, a short but profound and beautiful recitation imbued with his own deep scholarship and gnostic insights. He declared, 'I have received three *barakat* from Allah: to wear beautiful clothes, to eat beautiful food, and to perform beautiful *dhikr*.'[124]

WHO WAS THIS SHAYKH?

2. Shaykh Muhammad ibn al-Habib ad-Darqawi[125]

His noble lineage

The lineage of Sufi shaykh Muhammad ibn al-Habib ibn as-Siddiq al-Amghari al-Idrisi al-Hasani goes back to Shaykh 'Abdullah Amghar who is buried at Tamsloht near Marrakech, himself a descendant of a line which goes back to al-Hasan ibn 'Ali (d.680). His branch of the family emigrated to Tafilalat and settled there and then his father emigrated to Fes, settled there and members of his family still live there.

---

124   Abdalqadir as-Sufi, *The Diwan of Shaykh Ibn al-Habib*, Madinah Press (2001)

125   'Ali al-Jamal al-'Amrani, *The Meaning of Man: The Foundations of the Science of Knowledge*, op. cit., p.196

2. Chapter One: The Habibiyya Darqawiyya Order

His birth and primary education[126]

He was born in Fes, the cradle of knowledge and wellspring of spirituality, in 1295/1876. At the appropriate age, he went to the Qur'anic *kuttab* at Qantara Abu'r-Ru'us in the Sharabiliyyin quarter where he studied with the *faqih* and righteous *wali*, Sidi al-Hashimi as-Sanhaji, learning the basics of reading and writing and recitation of the Noble Qur'an. He also studied those things with the *faqih* Sidi Ahmad al-Filali in the elementary school of Qasba an-Nawwar and memorised the Qur'an under him.

In 1894 in the Abu'l-Junud Mosque in Fes he studied the *Ajrumiyya* by Ibn Ajrum as-Sanhaji (d. 1323), the *Alfiyya* by Imam Jamal ad-Deen ibn Malik (d. 1274) and then *Shama'il ar-Rasul* by at-Tirmidhi (d. 892). After that he studied the *Mukhtasar Khalil* by Khalil ibn Ishaq al-Jundi (d. 1365) and *at-Tuhfa* with the commentary of Shaykh at-Tawdi ibn Suda. He studied a part of *Sahih al-Bukhari* and the *Hikam* of Ibn 'Ata'allah as-Sakandari (d. 1310) with Shaykh Muhammad Ganun in the Qarawiyyin mosque in Fes. He also studied *Sahih al-Bukhari*, *ash-Shifa* of Qadi 'Iyad, the commentary on *al-Murshid al-Mu'in* by Mayyara and other primary texts with major scholars such as Shaykh 'Ahdullah ibn Idris al-Badrawi, Shaykh Muhammad as-Sanhaji and Muhammad ibn 'Abd ar-Rahman al-Filali.

His teachings[127]

In 1901 he finished his studies and began to teach on a voluntary basis in the mosque of Qasba an-Nawwar in Fes, teaching *al-Murshid al-Mu'in*, *al-Mukhtasar* of Khalil, *al-Muwatta'* of Imam Malik, and *tafsir*.

In 1936 he moved to Meknes where he continued his teaching in the Zaytuna Mosque, giving lessons in *tafsir*, and *fiqh* using the *Risala* of Ibn Abi Zayd al-Qayrawani. In his teaching of Sufism, he used *al-Hikam*, *al-Murshid al-Mu'in* and *ash-Shifa*.

---

126 http://en.wikipedia.org/wiki/Muhammad_ibn_al-Habib
127 http://en.wikipedia.org/wiki/Muhammad_ibn_al-Habib

His journeys and his ijazas[128]

Shaykh Muhammad ibn al-Habib ad-Darqawi received a number of scholarly *ijazas*, both written and oral. From Damascus he had a written *ijaza* from Shaykh Badr ad-Din ad-Dimashqi and another from Tlemcen from the Qadi, Abu Shu'ayb, and oral *ijazas* from Ahmad ibn al-Jilali al-Amghari and Abu Bakr ibn al-'Arabi Bannani.

In 1972 he left Meknes, the erstwhile imperial capital, to go to Makka to fulfil the duty of the hajj for the third time. On the way he stopped in one of his *zawiyyas* in Blida in Algeria where he died on 10th January 1972. He was buried there on the same day. Then, on 31st January of the same year, he was reburied in Meknes in his *zawiyya* in Darb al-Pasha close to the well-known Zaytuna mosque .

His works

We find that the most important extant work of Shaykh Muhammad ibn al-Habib ad-Darqawi is his *Diwan*, containing, among other things, a number of *qasidas* he composed on Sufism, good character and praise of Allah and praise of the Messenger ﷺ and religious teachings. It has been published at least twice in Arabic and also in English. A complete translation in English was published by Madinah Media, which is connected to the Sufi Habibiyya Daraqwiyya order of Ian Dallas. He also wrote a commentary on the prayer of Ibn Mashish.

His Sufism

Shaykh Muhammad ibn al-Habib was a Darqawi in the Badawi line and he received *idhn* for teaching and giving spiritual guidance from Shaykh Muhammad ibn 'Ali, buried in Marrakech, who took it from Shaykh al-'Arabi al-Huwari from Shaykh Muhammad al-'Arabi from Shaykh Ahmad al-Badawi from Shaykh al-'Arabi ad-Darqawi. His rank in Sufism, according to his people, reached that of the Qutb since "His secrets, his states, and his transmission were subtle and unsurpassed in the whole history of Sufism."[129] "The first proof is the perfection of his state in

---

128 http://en.wikipedia.org/wiki/Muhammad_ibn_al-Habib

129 Abdalqadir as-Sufi, *The Diwan of Shaykh Ibn al-Habib*, op. cit., preface

2. Chapter One: The Habibiyya Darqawiyya Order

every situation, his balance, deep wisdom, and continual trust in Allah. Everything turned around him, but he, in the centre of all the activity that surrounded him, turned only around his own heart, glorifying Allah with every breath."[130] "He said of himself, referring to his early years as a Sufi when he taught Arabic at the Qarawiyyin in Fez: "My station when I taught at the Qarawiyyin was equal to the station of Moulay 'Abdalqadir al-Jilani."[131]

When you consider his achievement in reviving the Darqawi *tariqa* and steering it through the difficult years of his time, you realise the stature of the man, the force of his religious personality and his vital position in the history of Sufism in Morocco, especially during the first half of the twentieth century, when "The Darqawi men were slaughtered and tortured by the colonial French occupation forces under the fanatical catholic leadership of the governor of Morocco (General Liauty)."[132] When the French left, the modernist and statist élite, who took over in the name of national freedom, continued the persecution. "These men were a threat because you could not build a consumer-state if there existed men who pointed out that if you were a consumer, you would be consumed."[133]

The most important achievement of Shaykh Muhammad ibn al-Habib is the great expansion of his *tariqa*, which continued, indeed increased, after his death. Shaykh Muhammad ibn al-Habib said to one of his *murids*, "All the *awliya'* have miracles, but the great *awliya's* miracles come after their deaths. Wait and you will see."[134] Ian Dallas says commenting on these words, "One of the miracles of the Shaykh has been that directly by his teaching and patience and supplication to Allah, Islam has spread dramatically in England, Spain and the United States."[135]

---

130 Ibid., preface

131 Abdalqadir as-Sufi, *The Diwan of Shaykh Ibn al-Habib*, op. cit., preface

132 'Ali al-Jamal al-'Amrani, *The Meaning of Man: The Foundations of the Science of Knowledge*, op. cit., p.3 (from the introduction of Abdalqadir as-Sufi)

133 Ibid.

134 Abdalqadir as-Sufi, *The Diwan of Shaykh Ibn al-Habib*, Madinah Press (2001)

135 Ibid.

Perhaps Ian Dallas means that the miracle of Shaykh Muhammad ibn al-Habib, which manifested after his death, is in fact himself, because, as he states, he was the one with *idhn* after him and the heir of his secret which he took to the West, especially to Britain. However, the matter of the inheritance of Shaykh Muhammad ibn al-Habib remains a subject of dispute among the *murids* of the Habibiyya order in Morocco, some of whom have given *bay'a* to Shaykh Moulay Hashim al-Belghayti, considering him to be the only one suited to take on the task of spiritual teaching after Shaykh Muhammad ibn al-Habib ad-Darqawi.

TOPIC TWO
THE WESTERN HABIBIYYA DARQAWIYYA ORDER

1. FOREWORD

The Habibiyya Darqawiyya order is now led in the West by Shaykh Abdalqadir as-Sufi, also known as 'Abdalqadir al-Murabit, who has also published books under the name of "Ian Dallas". He was appointed by his Shaykh Muhammad ibn al-Habib as the *muqaddim* of the Habibiyya Darqawiyya *tariqa* in the West but, sometime after the shaykh's death, he proclaimed himself as a shaykh of the order to convey it to the West. He moved to the British city of Norwich where his Sufi teachings began to take on new dimensions, although it continued to preserve its essential Moroccan roots and Darqawi characteristics.

2. SHAYKH ABDALQADIR AS-SUFI AL-MURABIT "IAN DALLAS"

A. Biography

The Scottish Shaykh Abdalqadir as-Sufi was born Ian Neil Dallas in 1931. Dallas, who was for a time the editor of *The International Times*, was a playwright and actor, playing the role of the magician in the seminal Fellini film 8½. He discovered Sufism through journeys to North Africa where, in 1967, he embraced Islam at the hand of Abdalkarim Daoudi, the *imam al-khatib* of the Qarawiyyin mosque in Fes. In 1968 he was initiated into Sufism by Shaykh Muhammad ibn al-Habib ad-Darqawi (1876-1972).

2. Chapter One: The Habibiyya Darqawiyya Order

He was appointed *muqaddim* by Shaykh Ibn al-Habib to represent him in the West and establish the order in his homeland, Britain. But after the death of the Shaykh of the Habibiyya order in 1972, Ian Dallas began to look for a new Shaykh and in 1976 he met Shaykh Hammuda al-Fayturi, the shaykh of the 'Alawiyya ad-Darqawiyya in Libya. Shaykh al-Fayturi appointed Ian Dallas shaykh of the Habibiyya and 'Alawiyya branches of the Darqawiyya *tariqa*, which he believed would be united under him.[136]

So in 1976 Ian Dallas ('Abdalqadir as-Sufi) proclaimed himself in England shaykh of the Habibiyya order and established a centre in the city of Norwich for his followers in the West, most of them young Britons and Americans who had become Muslim through him. In 1973 he had travelled to the U.S.A. to open the first of his centres there in Berkeley, California. Over the years other centres were established in almost every part of the U.S.A. (Texas, Georgia, Washington, California) and the *tariqa* has spread to most parts of the world (England, Spain, Malaysia, Germany, Nigeria, Australia, Switzerland, South Africa, Mexico and Denmark).[137]

'Abdalqadir as-Sufi al-Murabit has continued, down to the present time, to strengthen the presence of his order throughout the world. This has taken place despite some internal conflicts which affected the community as a result of its expansion, the autocratic role of the shaykh, and the attempts of the community to impose its political, economic and religious ideas. The American scholar Marcia Hermansen says, in a statement containing several inaccuracies, about the Murabitun movement of 'Abdalqadir as-Sufi:

"The Murâbitûn community convulsed in about 1983, principally due to problems with Abdalqadir's leadership as he sought to reduce the autonomy of the regional amîrs he had appointed. Some sources claim that internal dissension arose due to financial

---

136 Abdul Wahab el-Affendi, "A False Dawn" in Inquiry Magazine (January 1998): p.54

137 Fatima Harrak, "Le Soufisme Face A La Mondialisation: Cas Des Confréries D'Origine Africaine Aux USA" dans: Confréries Soufis d'Afrique: Nouveaux Rôles: Nouveaux Enjeux, 2004, Actes du Colloque International, Organise par l'Institut des Etudes Africaines Rabat, 2-4 Octobre 2001, p.191

scandal and abuses of polygamy:..."[138] as "...his leadership became more and more autocratic. At one point he commanded all his followers to sell their cars, at another to divorce their wives."[139]

But these criticisms cannot conceal the real successes which the Habibiyya Darqawiyya order has achieved under his command in the West. It brought the message of Islam in full (its spiritual reality and its legal modality) to regions far from the Islamic world, including currently Mexico and Latin America. It has also reinvigorated the spiritual legacy of the Muslims in the Western world. It is enough to point out that it has built a mosque in the heart of al-Andalus after 500 years of silence,[140] a mosque in the Albaicin in the ancient city of Granada, which will strive, according to its directors who are among the leaders of the Habibiyya order in the West:

> "To encourage the exchange of shared knowledge and action with the rest of the Muslims of Europe with the aim of forging a new Islamic identity in the ancient continent. ... It aims to form a connecting link between the Muslims in Granada and Spain and the rest of Europe. As well as its primary aim, which is the establishment of the prayer, it has an extensive program of activities through its Islamic centre which adjoins it. This centre contains many facilities and concentrates on regular activities, as announced by the Mosque foundation, to make Islam better known among non-Muslims and also to provide ongoing teaching for Muslims so as to make it a nucleus for the daily life of Muslim immigrants in Granada".[141]

---

138 Marcia Hermansen, "The 'Other' Shadhilis of the West" in *The Shadhiliyya*, op. cit., p.490

139 Ibid. p.487

140 This is the title of an article written by: Mustafa Malak, in: Azzaman Magazine, No.1561 (July 20, 2003).

141 Mustafa Malak, "*Masjid fi Qalbi al-Hayyi al-Andalussiyyi al-'Atiq Ba'da 500 'Am Mina Samt: Man Yanfudhu al-Ghubara 'An Thaqafati al-Islamiyyati fi Isbaniya*", in: Azzaman Magazine. No.1561 (July 20, 2003)

2. Chapter One: The Habibiyya Darqawiyya Order

CHAIN OF ISNAD CHART[142]

In the Name of Allah the Merciful the Compassionate

Sayyiduna
Muhammad
blessings and peace of Allah be upon him
|
Sayyiduna 'Ali ibn Abi Talib

Sayyidi al-Hasan ibn 'Ali	In the Name of Allah, the Merciful, the Compassionate. Say: 'He is Allah, One. Allah, as-Samad. He has not begotten, nor was he begotten, and no-one is like Him.'	Sayyidi al-Hasan al-Basri
Sayyidi Abu Muhammad Jabir		Sayyidi Habib al-'Ajami
Sayyidi Sa'id al-Gharwani		Sayyidi Da'ud at-Ta'i
Sayyidi Fathu's-Su'ud		Sayyidi Ma'ruf al-Karkhi
Sayyidi Sa'd		Sayyidi as-Sari as-Saqti
Sayyidi Sa'id		Al-Imam al-Junayd
Sayyidi Ahmad al-Marwani		Sayyidi ash-Shibli
Sayyidi Ibrahim al-Basri		Sayyidi at-Tartusi
Sayyidi Zaynu'd-Din al-Qazwini		Sayyidi Abu'l-Hasan al-Hakkari
Sayyidi Muhammad Shamsu'd-Din		Sayyidi Abu Sa'id al-Mubarak
Sayyidi Muhammad Taju'd-Din		Mawlana 'Abdal-Qadir al-Jilani
Sayyidi Nuru'd-Din Abu'l-Hasan 'Ali		Sayyidi Abu Madyan al-Ghawth
Sayyidi Fakhuru'd-Din		Sayyidi Muhammad Salih
Sayyidi Tuqayyu'd-Din		Sayyidi Muhammad ibn Harazim
Sayyidi 'Abd ar-Rahman al-'Attar		

Sayyidi 'Abdu's-Salam ibn Mashish
Sayyidi Abu'l-Hasan ash-Shadhili
Sayyidi Abu'l Abbas al-Mursi
Sayyidi Ahmad ibn 'Ata'Illah
Sayyidi Da'ud al-Bakhili
Sayyidi Muhammad Wafa
Sayyidi 'Ali Wafa
Sayyidi Yahya al-Qadiri
Sayyidi Ahmad al-Hadrami
Sayyidi Ahmad az-Zarruq
Sayyidi Ibrahim al-Fahham
Sayyidi 'Ali ad-Dawwar
Sayyidi 'Abd ar-Rahman al-Majdhub
Sayyidi Yusuf al-Fasi
Sayyidi 'Abdu'r-Rahman al-Fasi
Sayyidi Muhammad ibn 'Abdillah
Sayyidi Qasim al-Khassasi
Sayyidi Ahmad ibn 'Abdillah
Sayyidi al-'Arabi ibn 'Abdillah
Sayyidi 'Ali al-Jamal
Mawlay al-'Arabi ibn Ahmad ad-Darqawi

The Chain of Teachers of the Shadhiliyya – Darqawiyya – Habibiyya Tariqa from their source, may the blessings and peace of Allah be upon him, up to the present day.

And there came from the farthest part of the city a man running. He said, 'O my people, follow those who have been sent.'

Sayyidi Abu Ya'za al-Muhaji	Sayyidi Ahmad al-Badawi
Sayyidi Muhammad ibn 'Abd al-Qadir al-Basha	Sayyidi Muhammad al-'Arabi
Sayyidi Muhammad ibn Qidur	Sayyidi al-'Arabi al-Hawwari
Sayyidi ibn al-Habib al-Buzidi	Sayyidi Muhammad ibn 'Ali
Mawlana Ahmadibn Mustafa al-'Alawi	Sayyidi Muhammad ibn al-Habib
Sayyidi Muhammad al-Fayturi Hamuda	

Sayyidi 'Abd al-Qadir as-Sufi ad-Darqawi al-Murabit

---

142 'Ali al-Jamal al-'Amrani, *The Meaning of Man: The Foundations of the Science of Knowledge*, op. cit., p.442

TOPIC THREE
THE PATH FOLLOWED BY THE WESTERN HABIBIYYA ORDER AND ITS TRANSFORMATION INTO THE WORLDWIDE MURABITUN MOVEMENT

1. THE PATH OF THE WESTERN HABIBIYYA ORDER

Someone who follows the life of Shaykh Abdalqadir ad-Sufi will be able to pick out two distinct stages in his *da'wah* activity. The first is a purely Sufic approach and the second is mixed with political and economic activity. Ali Kose distinguishes two phases in the teachings of Shaykh Abdalqadir beginning with an earlier esoteric Sufic period favouring isolation from society and later entering an active political phase.[143] "These transitions may be traced in his writings which develop from *The Book of Strangers* by Ian Dallas, a mystical quest novel, to *The Way of Muhammad* by Abdal al-Qadir as-Sufi to *Jihad: A Groundplan*, to *The Sign of the Sword* by Shaykh Abdalqadir al-Murabit, and more recently to *Letter to an Arab Muslim* and *Technique of the Coup de Banque*."[144]

2. THE MURABITUN AND REFORM ACTIVITIES

The Murabitun are the second phase of the development of the Habibiyya Darqawiyya order in the West. Shaykh Abdalqadir adopted this name in 1983 in honour of the Murabitun dynasty of Morocco who were known for their support of Islam and strong adherence to Maliki *fiqh* and jihad, especially in al-Andalus. Marcia Hermansen says about this: "The name Murâbitûn evokes the *ribât* as a site of separation from the surrounding '*jâhil*' culture. *Ribât* means a fortress on the frontiers of Islâm and resonates with the legacy of the North African Murâbitûn movement of the 11th century where jihad was combined with extreme religious piety."[145] She further comments: "The Sufi movement of

---

143   Ali Kose, *Conversion to Islam: A study of Native British Converts*, London: Kegan Paul, (1996), p.181

144   Marcia Hermansen, "The 'Other' Shadhilis of the West" in *The Shadhiliyya*, op. cit., p.488

145   Marcia Hermansen, "The 'Other' Shadhilis of the West" in *The Shadhiliyya*, op. cit., p.489

Abdalqadir as-Sufi became increasingly rigid and cultlike, adopting the name 'the Murâbitûn' in 1983, and minting their own gold coins to try and avoid the contamination of the interest-based international banking system."[146]

The movement concentrated on teaching its followers a firm legal foundation, based on the Maliki school, by promoting the study of the *Muwatta'* of Imam Malik as the basis for an ideal social and legal modality, while beginning to concentrate less on the inward teachings of Sufism. Study of the *Muwatta'* convinced 'Abdalqadir as-Sufi to stress financial reform and a return to pristine Islamic practice, including upholding the validity of slavery, within its proper context – as he stipulated in his book, *The Sign of the Sword* – the re-imposition of the obligation of *jizya*, *ghazwa*, slavery and spoils of war as elements of jihad.[147]

3. CONTROVERSIAL AREAS

A. Dealings with banks and financial activity

Among the widely-debated controversies, which the Habibiyya order and Shaykh Abdalqadir as-Sufi have provoked, is regarding the matter of the forbidding and absolute prohibition of dealing with the existing usury-based economic system. That is found in a fatwa which Hajj 'Umar Vadillo issued, based on the command of Shaykh Abdalqadir.[148] This prohibition includes the use of prevailing paper currencies such as the American dollar and Euro. To replace them he advocated a new medium of exchange based on bi-metal (silver and gold) coinage which became a physical reality after the first gold dinar was minted in 2000 by the Islamic Mint which is controlled by the Murabitun and is based in Dubai. Vadillo considers the issuance of the dinar to be a major opening for the Islamic nation and a strong sign of the collapse of Western hegemonic capitalism when he says: "The return of the gold dinar to the world's economies

---

146   Ibid. p.489

147   Abdalqadir al-Murabit, *The Sign of The Sword*, pp.48-84

148   Umar Ibrahim Vadillo, "Fatwa on Banking: And the Use of Interest Received on Bank Deposits" on webpage: http://www.shaykhabdalqadir.com/content/articles/FatwaOnBanking.pdf, viewed:10/08/2007

would be the single most unifying event for Muslims in the modern era.... Shortly afterwards, the capitalist structure will quickly fall and will make the Wall Street crash of 1929 seem minor by comparison".[149]

Some look at his project as an "Islamic bomb" which "could pose a threat to the U.S. dollar and the existing world order."[150] 'Abdalqadir as-Sufi wrote a preface to the book of Umar Vadillo, his right hand man in this project, *The Return of the Gold Dinar*. He says in it: "There is no doubt that this work puts behind it a century of suffering and defeat for the Muslims and opens the coming age to a powerful and revived Islam."[151] Some Western politicians countered it but the project began to be endorsed by Islamist political figures such as Malaysia's Mohamad Mahaththir and Turkey's Necmettin Erbakan, and some local Indonesian governors.[152]

B. Positions on politics and creed

Anyone who follows the development of the Habibiyya order in the West will notice that, in this last phase, it has become more involved in global political and religious debates without concentrating on any particular region, although critical regions such as Palestine, Iraq and Pakistan are frequently mentioned in the almost monthly essays which the Shaykh issues on his website, including "Pakistan in Crisis", "The Lebanon Crisis I", "The Lebanon Crisis II", "Iraq – Killing Field of the Kuffar", "British Elections", "Spain – Civil War And Isma'ili War" and also "Democracy and Finance – the Axis of Evil" and "On Terrorism" and a large number of other topics.[153] All of them are, however, unified by an implacable opposition to the West's injustice towards Islam, to some Arab leaders' attacks against their religion and their community,

---

149 A talk delivered by Umar Vadillo at a conference entitled "Islam in Europe" which took place in Granada, Spain 11th July, 2003

150 Jay Taylor, "The Islamic (Gold) Dinar" in Gold-Eagle 30th Nov/1998 according to Marcia Hermansen, "The 'Other' Shadhilis of the West" in *The Shadhiliyya*, op. cit. p.491

151 See the introduction to the book.

152 Marcia Hermansen, "The 'Other' Shadhilis of the West" in *The Shadhiliyya*, op. cit., p.491

153 http://www.shaykhabdalqadir.com/content/articles.html

2. Chapter One: The Habibiyya Darqawiyya Order

and especially to the enemy which has occupied the land of the Aqsa Mosque, the Jews of Israel, which has made some accuse him of Anti-Semitism. The fact that he has spoken about the political role of the Jews in modern usury-based finance, that he refused to classify the Nazi Hitler as "the metaphysical embodiment of evil"[154] and that he supported the Palestinian *Intifada* in general, was something which led Jews, especially Israelis, to attack him and shun his movement.

He has adopted a similar strong position in his essays dealing with religious doctrine in which he has attacked Wahhabis and criticised their stance towards Sufism, an example being his essay entitled "The Wahhabis and the Sufis".[155] He has excluded groups which have adopted jihadi thought, such as the al-Qa'ida movement, from the circle of the people of the Sunna and the Community. His repudiation of Sufi groups which espouse Universalism or Perennial philosophy, such as the followers of Frithjof Schuon, René Guenon and Martin Lings, is well known, as is his repudiation of those who espouse Mahdism, such as the people of Shaykh Hisham Kabbani[156] and his shaykh Nazim al-Haqqani.[157] This has resulted in a reaction from these groups accusing him and his movement of extremism and belonging to the Kharijites and of being hostile to the people of Allah and His righteous *awliya*,[158] accusations of untruthfulness and even of *takfir*.[159]

Although Shaykh Abdalqadir and his Sufi group try to build a serious

154 Abdalqadir as-Sufi, *Technique of the Coup de Banque*, (p.35) on website: http://www.scribd.com/doc/14344614/Coup-De-banque

155 See this article on the website of Shaykh Abdalqadir as-Sufi: http://www.shaykhabdalqadir.com/content/articles.htm

156 Shaykh Hisham Kabbani is the representative of the Naqshabandi Haqqani *zawiyah* in North America and the deputy and son-in-law of its Turkish shaykh Nazim al-Haqqani.

157 Umar Ibrahim Vadillo, *The Esoteric Deviation in Islam*, op. cit.

158 G. F. Haddad, "The Murabitun & Shaykh Nazim al-Haqqani: Refutation of Umar Vadillo's The Esoteric Deviation in Islam" in: http://www.sunnah.org/publication/salafi/vadillo/murabitun.htm

159 Omar K. Neusser, "Defense against Slander and *Takfir* Coming from the 'Murabitun' Movement as an Example for Sects in General" in: http://www.livingislam.org/o/dstm_e.html

dialogue with the Christians, the issue of criticizing Pope Benedict II criticising the Prophet Muhammad ﷺ undermined these efforts and made Shaykh Abdalqadir issue a fatwa, published on his website, accusing the Pope of having been a Nazi, and the church of usurious transactions and malice towards Islam.[160]

TOPIC FOUR
THE BRANCHES OF THE WESTERN HABIBIYYA DARQAWIYA ORDER

The sources we have relied on in our research have not facilitated the study of all the branches of the Habibiyya order nor the reasons and circumstances behind the splitting off of some groups from it despite retaining a connection to Shaykh Abdalqadir as-Sufi. Nor do they help us dispel the fog which obscures the identity of some of the groups connected to the Habibiyya order. One of the most important of these is the Haydariyya Shadhiliyya order or the Ja'fariyya order.

1. THE SHADHILIYYA HAYDARIYYA ORDER OF FADHLALLA HAERI

A. Foreword

The shaykh of this group, Fadhlalla Haeri, comes from an Iraqi family of Shi'ite scholars. He was affiliated for a time with Shaykh Abdalqadir al-Sufi al-Murabit and the Habibiyya Darqawiyya order during the late 1970s and the early 1980s. Fadlullah Haeri then formed an independent Sufi group at the beginning of the 1980s, after which he worked to expand his network of Sufi centres in different regions of the world. He sent his *murids* to Latin America and to some Pakistani towns.[161]

Regarding the identity of the *tariqa*, Fadhlalla maintains that he represents the Ja'fariyya Shadhiliyya *tariqa*. He said in this context, "We are Shadhilis, but our *tariqa* is Ja'fari-Shadhiliyya because I am a Ja'fari. On the haqiqa

---

160 See this fatwa at the following address: http://www.shaykhabdalqadir.com/content/articles.html

161 Marcia Hermansen, "The 'Other' Shadhilis of the West" in *The Shadhiliyya*, op. cit., p. 491

2. Chapter One: The Habibiyya Darqawiyya Order

side we are 'Alawis, Muhammadi, and finally Allahîs, waiting for death."[162] Muneera Haeri, the wife of Fadhlalla and a Muslim of Scottish descent, published a book about the Chishti order (2001) in which she claimed that Fadhlalla is a Chishti shaykh, further complicating the identity of this *tariqa*.[163] Another factor further obscuring its identity is the connection of the order of Fadhlalla to Iranian Sufism since, as the American scholar Marcia Hermansen indicates: "Some statements strongly convey Fadhlalla's preservation of his Shi'ite identity such as when he says that he received support from some members of the Iranian royal family and the fact that his lectures in Pakistan are given in Shi'a social centers".[164]

This assertion is difficult to corroborate as Hermansen presented her information in an unsubstantiated way without giving any reliable source for it. There is also an essential difficulty presented by the fact that there are, in any case, some questions about the compatibility of Sufism and Shi'ism. The Moroccan scholar 'Abd as-Salam al-Gharmini says: "The basic doctrines of Shi'ism contain elements which are incompatible with Sufism, because Shi'ism gives absolute ascendancy to the progeny of Fatima az-Zuhra. This means the ranks of perfection are confined by them to the descendants of 'Ali, whereas we find that the Sufis, despite a teaching founded on great love for the family of the Prophet ﷺ, do not restrict perfection in either character or spiritual rank to them alone, seeing it rather as a possibility for any human being. Lineage is not a precondition for either acceptability or perfection. The ethos of Shi'ism also contains another element which conflicts with the previous assertion. Upholding the ascendancy of the 'Alawis and love for them also entails rejection of many of the First Community and denunciation of them, or rather hatred of them, regarding the disagreement surrounding the imamate, the position of the people of the Sunna and other essential matters".[165]

---

162 Fadhlallah Haeri, *Songs of Iman on the Roads of Pakistan: Talks Given During a Tour of Pakistan*, Zahra Publications, Blanco, TX, U.S.A (1983) p.108

163 Marcia Hermansen, "The 'Other' Shadhilis of the West" in *The Shadhiliyya*, op. cit., p. 492

164 Ibid. p. 491

165 Al-Gharmini, 'Abd-Salam. *as-Sufi wa al-Akhar: Dirasat Naqdiyya fi al-Fikr*

B. The life of Shaykh Fadhlalla Haeri

Fadhlalla Haeri is an Iraqi Shi'ite Muslim engineer, who was born in Karbala and went to the West at an early age to pursue his studies.[166] He joined the group of Abdalqadir as-Sufi (the Habibiyya) during the late 1970s. In 1979 he settled in the U.S.A. with the aim of founding a centre of Islamic teaching, working together with Shaykh Abad al-Qadir as-Sufi. In 1980 he founded an organisation called the Zahra Trust[167] in Blanco, Texas, a town near the city of San Antonio. In 1981 it began to take shape with the building of a school and mosque as the core of a community known as Bayt ad-Deen, which aspired to model itself on the first Islamic community in Madina. In the winter of 1981 Fadhlalla Haeri held there the first Sufi gathering of Bayt ad-Deen.[168] However, at the end of the 1980s[169] he decided to move his Sufi order to England, the rumoured cause of the move being financial irregularities.

C. His works and books

Fadhlalla Haeri has published a number of books dealing with Sufi thought and Qur'anic interpretation. His studies dealing with Sufism have been widely disseminated since large publishing houses have competed to publish them, and they have been reprinted several times. Some of his major works are:

1. *Beginning's End*
2. *Commentary on the Qur'an*
3. *Cosmology of the Self*
4. *Eid Talk*

---

al-Islami al-Muqarin. Al-Madaress for Print and Publication: Casablanca, 1st edition (2000CE/1421 AH), pp.149-150

166 Marcia Hermansen, "The 'Other' Shadhilis of the West" in *The Shadhiliyya*, op. cit., p. 491

167 *Nuradeen, An Islamic Sufi Journal: Selections* (Blanco, Texas: Zahra Publications, 1983)

168 "Bayt al-Deen: An Experiment," Nuradeen 2 (No.4, Autumn 1992):26-27

169 Marcia Hermansen, "In the Garden of American Sufi Movements: Hybrids and Perennials," in *New Trends and Developments in the World of Islam*, ed. Peter Clarke, London: Luzac Oriental Press, 1997, p. 170

5. *Forty Windows and More*
6. *Journey of the Universe as Expounded in the Qur'an*
7. *Living Islam East and West*
8. *Poems*
9. *Ripples of Light*
10. *Seven Patterns of the Self*
11. *The Elements of Islam*
12. *The Elements of Sufism*
13. *The Inner Meanings of Worship in Islam*
14. *The Journey of the Self*
15. *The Light, Love and Peace of Islam*
16. *The Pilgrimage of Islam*
17. *The Wisdom of Ibn Ata'Allah*
18. *Calling Allah by His Most Beautiful Names*
19. *Son of Karbala'*
20. *Witnessing Perfection*
21. *The Thoughtful Guide to Islam*

2. THE GROUP OF SHAYKH MARK HANSON (HAMZA YUSUF)

A. Foreword

The American scholar Marcia Hermansen says about him: "Perhaps the most prominent example is Shaykh Hamza Yusuf, a popular American Muslim teacher with global popularity among Muslim youth, who was a disciple of Abdalqadir until about 1983."[170]

Despite the fact that Mark Hanson has not founded a particular order which bears his name, he has a distinct pedagogical and religious orientation and has followers and *murids* spread throughout various areas of the world, especially in Western countries. Who is this Shaykh? How does he express his Islamic teaching currently in the West?

---

170 Marcia Hermansen, "The 'Other' Shadhilis of the West" in *The Shadhiliyya*, op. cit., p. 491

B. The life of Shaykh Mark Hanson (Hamza Yusuf)

Hamza Yusuf was born in 1960 in the state of Washington into a Greek Orthodox family and was brought up in northern California. He entered university in the philosophy faculty where he became acquainted with various ideas about Islam and the East. He then met some black American Muslims who had a strong effect on him and he decided to investigate the Islamic religion. In 1977, at the age of 17, he embraced Islam in Santa Barbara in California and then, after spending some years in the company of Shaykh Abdalqadir as-Sufi, he travelled in the Muslim world. He studied the Islamic religion and Arabic language for some time in the U.A.E. and Saudi Arabia and then he travelled to West Africa to study and became a student of six shaykhs and scholars in Morocco, Mauritania and Algeria.

During this period he received many teaching *ijazas* and diplomas in branches of knowledge of the Shari'a from Muslim teaching institutions. After ten years study abroad, he returned to the U.S.A. to obtain a higher degree in religious studies from the University of San Jose. He is now considered to be one the most important teachers and Sufi missionaries in America and the Western world in general. He is remarkably active and very popular in the U.S.A. and elsewhere, and concentrates on demonstrating the integral connection between Islam and Sufism.

After his return to the U.S.A., in 1996 he founded the Zaytuna Institute in California, which is dedicated to the revival of Islamic Sciences and the preservation of traditional teaching methods.[171] This institute has a significant international reputation due to the excellence of the clear picture of Sufi Islam it presents to the West. This caused its leader, Hamza Yusuf, to be asked by the British Parliament to present the Islamic viewpoint on a number of current world issues, such as terrorism and extremism. He also appeared beside the American President George Bush directly after the events of 11 September 2001,[172] something which exposed him to a some criticism, making some describe him – as the noted British newspaper the

---

171   http://www.zaytuna.org/teacherMore.asp?id=9, viewed: 20/07/2007

172   http://www.guardian.co.uk/g2/story/0,3604,564960,00.html#article_continue, published: Monday, October 8, 2001

2. Chapter One: The Habibiyya Darqawiyya Order

Guardian – did as "Bush's pet Muslim".[173] Other western voices described him as "the Sufi Master of Deceit".[174]

Some distinguishing features of Shaykh Mark Hanson (Hamza Yusuf) are that:

- he is as proficient in Arabic as he is in English and has memorised a lot of poetry and stories. This means that he can speak to Westerners in a language they understand and to Arab Muslims in a language which they do.
- he strives to convey a picture of flexible and open Islamic Sufism to remove the distorted picture which the West has of Islam and Muslims.
- he has many connections with American and European Muslims in the Western world, including Shaykh Abdalqadir as-Sufi, and had a strong connection with Martin Lings, especially in the final years of his life.[175]
- he has a distinct media presence, exemplified by the successful programme known as "A Journey with Hamza Yusuf" which went out over three consecutive years on the Arabic-language satellite channel, MBC.[176]

Shaykh Mark Hanson is also thought to be the first American to teach in the ancient Qarawiyyin mosque in the city of Fes in Morocco[177] and he has made a number of translations of *qasidas* and classical texts from Arabic to modern English.[178] He has also travelled to many parts of the world lecturing on the spiritual aspects of Islam and contemporary issues. He currently resides in northern California with his wife and five children.

---

173 Ibid.

174 Stephen Schwartz, "The 'Sufi' Master of Deceit: Hamza Yusuf Hanson" viewed: 25/08/2007 in: http://www.familysecuritymatters.org/global.php?id=881447

175 Hamza Yusuf, "Q-News", June(2005), No.363, p.53

176 http://sheikhhamza.com/biography_text.asp viewed: 28/08/2007

177 Ibid. viewed: 28/08/2007

178 http://en.wikipedia.org/wiki/Hamza_Yusuf#_note-0 viewed: 20/07/2007

C. His works and books

Among his translations:

1. *The Creed of Imam al-Tahawi* (238/853 – 321/933)
2. *Purification of the Heart: Signs, Symptoms and Cures of the Spiritual Diseases of the Heart*

His own books include:

1. *The State We Are In: Identity, Terror, and the Law of Jihad*
2. *Educating your child in Modern Times*

CHAPTER TWO

MOROCCAN INFLUENCE IN BRITAIN: THE WESTERN HABIBIYYA DARQAWIYYA ORDER AS A MODEL

FOREWORD

ONE OF THE most notable manifestations of Moroccan influence in the Habibiyya order of Shaykh Abdalqadir as-Sufi is its holding to Junaydi Sufism as well as the Ash'ari creed and Malik *fiqh*. These three are considered to be among the most important characteristics of Moroccan Sufism. Professor Muhammad Haji says in this context: "The Moroccans chose a Sufism of good character and *suluk*, following Imam al-Junayd, just as they chose the Ash'ari creed in theology and the school of Imam Malik in law. This choice itself is one of the characteristics of Moroccan Sufism, since, with the exception of a very small group, Moroccan Sufis have never immersed themselves in the investigation of arcane spiritual truths, complex spiritual states, ecstatic utterances or discussions about the unity of existence."[179]

Morocco has known Sufism throughout its Islamic period and its features first appeared with the arrival of the first conquerors, even if its actual and palpable existence only emerged at the time of the Murabitun state. The scholar 'Abd al-Wahhab al-Filali says: "Sufism is a prominent phenomenon in Morocco and a cultural given within Moroccan culture. Its time of emergence was the Murabitun period and it has developed over

[179] Muhammad Hajji, interviewed by: al-Ishara Newspaper, 2nd year, Vol. No.16 (April: 2001), p.4

the passage time since them. The movement of Sufism did not retreat in the 'Alawite era from its prior increase and so it demonstrated its staying power and increased presence by its undoubted effect on both practice and action and also on thought and creed".[180]

TOPIC ONE
THE MOROCCAN SUFI INFLUENCE ON THE WESTERN HABIBIYYA DARAQWIYYA ORDER

1. THE *JALALI* (MAJESTIC) PATH

Jalal (majesty) in this context does not imply the Sufic understanding of the word, entailing the movement of a *murid* to a state of astonishment, confusion and contraction as a result of the epiphany of majestic Divine Names. Rather it refers to the thought springing from the depths of the Sufi experience which results in a series of principles and means. These in turn produce a structure and ethos for the *murid* on the Sufic path and have a cultural and social influence on the environment in which he lives.

Majesty and beauty are connected in the Sufic context in both an intertwined and also a contrasting way. This causes them to alternate in some instances and to co-exist in others, which is the case in the particular context about which we are speaking. It is part of Sufi doctrine that majesty leads to the genesis of beauty and seals it with its specific form. That is how new thought is generated. So generation and reflection occur under one robe and they can either be connected and unified or separated and different.

A. The principles of Sufi reflection

The flexibility of Moroccan Sufi teachings and principles and their ability to adapt and harmonise with the Western environment are clearly demonstrated by what has happened in Britain where they are an

---

180 'Abdel-Wahhab El-Filali, *al-Adab As-Sufi fi al-Maghrib Ibbana al-Qarnayn 18&19 CE: Dhawahir wa Qadaya*, a thesis submitted for the fulfilment of the requirement of a Doctor in Philosophy in Arabic studies specialisation in Moroccan Literature. Sidi Muhammad ibn Abdullah University Dhahr Mihraz –Fez. Under the supervision of Doctor Ahmad al-'Iraqi (2000-2001CE/1421-1422AH), p.14

2. Chapter Two: Moroccan Influence in Britain

essential element of the programme of the Habibiyya Darqawiyya order of Ian Dallas. This order continues to preserve its original Darqawi form, reflected in the retention by Shaykh Abdalqadir as-Sufi of the same *wirds* and *dhikr* which he inherited from his predecessor, Shaykh Muhammad ibn al-Habib ad-Darqawi. It also appears in the form of its members' handshake, which maintains its Sufi Moroccan character by both parties kissing hands, as can be clearly seen in video clips on the website of Shaykh Abdalqadir as-Sufi.[181]

The connection with Darqawi Moroccan thought and experience has also been preserved by Shaykh Abdalqadir as-Sufi through his encouraging his followers and *murids* to continue to read the Morocan Sufi texts which contain the teaching of the *tariqa*. For example, we can mention the letters of Shaykh al-'Arabi ad-Darqawi, the letters of Shaykh 'Ali al-Jamal al-'Imrani, a collection of instructional Darqawi *qasidas*, the commentary on the prayer of the *Treasury of Truths* by Shaykh Muhammad ibn al-Habib ad-Darqawi, as well as other works and Moroccan Sufi texts. The western Habibiyya Darqawiyya order has translated and published these works in English with the aim of making the British *murids* firm in the Habibiyya order and making English-speaking regions of the Western world familiar with Sufi thought and practice.

B. Manifestations of the *jalali* form

Part of this *jalali* Moroccan effect on the western Habibiyya Darqawi order can be seen in their form of dress and their wearing of the *tasbih*. This marks out the followers of this order from their British environment in particular and the West in general. The British scholar Ron Greaves describes this phenomenon by saying: "The followers wear green turbans, Moroccan traditional dress."[182] It is known that green turbans, short *jalabas* and wearing the *tasbih* round the neck were distinctive features of the followers of the Darqawi order in Morocco. Shaykh Abdalqadir as-Sufi inherited these from his Moroccan shaykh and taught his followers that there was no harm in wearing them and going about dressed in this

---

181 http://www.shaykhabdalqadir.com/content/video.html

182 R. Geaves, *The Sufis of Britain: An Exploration of Muslim Identity* (Cardiff: Cardiff Academic Press, 2000), p.143

way. This can be seen in those pictures in which Shaykh Abdalqadir as-Sufi appears both alone, and with a group of his followers wearing Moroccan *jalabas* and with *tasbihs* around their necks.

2. THE *JAMALI* (BEAUTIFUL) PATH

Jamal (beauty) in this context does not imply the Sufic understanding of the word by which the *murid* on the path experiences a state of expansion when the Beautiful Divine Names are unveiled to him. What is meant by it is a manifestation of different types of literary expression, deriving from Sufi practice, taking the form of both poetry and prose, such as the biography of the Prophet ﷺ, and also songs and Sufi *dhikrs*, which serve as a means of teaching and generate spiritual experience in the heart of the *murid*.

A. The Sira of the Prophet ﷺ

Sufism is generally characterised by praise of the Messenger of Allah ﷺ in its teachings, but absolute love for the Messenger of Allah ﷺ is an intrinsically Moroccan phenomenon in which both the common and élite take part. It is, therefore, not surprising that we find that the Sufis of Morocco study the *sira* of the Prophet ﷺ in their *zawiyyas* with the aim of generating love for the Messenger of Allah ﷺ in their hearts. Perhaps the most important work they rely on to achieve this goal is the book *ash-Shifa bi-ta'rif huquq al-Mustafa* by the Moroccan scholar Qadi 'Iyad.

Ash-Shifa is one of the great books of Prophetic *sira* and the Sufis of Morocco give great importance to it because it relates the life of the Messenger of Allah ﷺ in a style brimming with love, yearning and connection to the reality of the Prophetic phenomenon. It records the miracles which occurred at the hand of the Messenger of Allah ﷺ among his Companions and in it there are important instructional indications from which *murids* can benefit and learn correct behaviour with regard to their relationship with their shaykhs and the Muhammadan and Divine presences. For this reason the Sufis of Morocco have a custom of gathering to study the book *ash-Shifa* by Qadi 'Iyad at least twice a year, for the celebration of the Night of Power and the Mawlud of the Prophet. Imitating the Sufis of Morocco, the Habibiyya order have preserved this

2. Chapter Two: Moroccan Influence in Britain

praiseworthy legacy and have upheld the special quality of this book. 'Abdalqadir has explained this by saying: "The *Shifa* of Qadi Iyad inspires essential internal love for the Messenger ﷺ and all that is necessary to complete the restoration of Islamic judgement."[183]

Love of the Messenger ﷺ, according to the belief of Shaykh Abdalqadir as-Sufi, represents the third element supporting the application of the Shari'a and the basis of the foundation of Islamic power. The Prophet ﷺ said, "By the One Who has my soul in His hand, none of you will believe until he loves me more than himself, his family and his possessions and all people."[184] Shaykh Abdalqadir says about this matter:

> "The means to this compassion and this *rahma* is the love of the Messenger of Allah, may Allah bless him and give him peace. And so for this we have selected a book of *sira*. As you know there is a vast *sira* literature, and we have selected a book which is very early, which is about a thousand years old, and which has in it no fantasy, no fabulous elements, no hagiography of exaltation and metaphysical speculation, but simply tells the wonderful story of the Messenger of Allah, may Allah bless him and give him peace ... We have taken the *Shifa'* of Qadi 'Iyad as the third book in this basic Islamic education. We have Qur'an al-Karim with *Tafsir Jalalayn*. We have *al-Muwatta'* of Imam Malik."[185]

Shaykh Abdalqadir summarises Qadi 'Iyad's book *ash-Shifa* by picking out three basic points. He says: "Firstly it says what Allah has said about him in His book. And these are not just the famous *ayats* that we know – "*Rahmatu'l-lil-'alameen*,"[186] and so on, but *ayats* which we do not recognise at first as connecting to the Messenger of Allah, Allah's blessings and peace be upon him, and that are in themselves an education and an inspiration for us. That is the first wonderful thing about this book. Secondly everything

---

[183] Abdalhaqq Bewley, "The Recovery of True Islamic Fiqh: An introduction to the work of Shaykh Abdalqadir as-Sufi", http://bewley.virtualave.net/saq.html/

[184] *Sahih al-Bukhari* 1/10, (15) and in *Sahih Muslim* 1/49 (44) (69) (70) according to Anas Ibn Malik

[185] Abdalqadir as-Sufi, *Root Islamic Education*, Ch. 1. On-line at http://bewley.virtualave.net viewed July 2007

[186] The Noble Quran: al-Anbiya 21:107

it says about him and that he has said about himself, and which his Sahaba have said, come from hadiths that have been scrutinised by its author, who is one of the greatest *muhaddithun* in the history of the science. And the third thing is that this book in its quality, is suffused with a love of the Prophet, peace be upon him, that is so overwhelming that you cannot read it without being affected. And the key to this is that the man who wrote the book was cutting heads, and hands, and marking backs, and passing sentences, and giving orders to Amirs. He was living it. He was on the edge. And he could not do it without help. He could not do it without the *rahma* of Allah. He could not do it without the *'ibada* that gave him great, great love of the Messenger, may Allah bless him and give him peace."[187]

B. *Sama'* and praise

Moroccan *sama'* is present in the Habibiyya Darqawiyya order as a primary instrument. Indeed it forms the core of all the types of *sama'* and religious songs which Shaykh Abdalqadir as-Sufi uses in his teaching, following the example of his Moroccan shaykh. One of the main forms this *sama'* takes is the singing of the *qasidas* in the Diwan of Shaykh Muhammad ibn al-Habib, *Bughya al-Muridin as-Sa'irin wa Tuhfa al-'arifin as-Salikin*. 'Abdalqadir as Sufi says in this context: "From this Diwan a new element was introduced into the practice of the Sufis. Where before the diwans were only sung at the gathering of *sama'*, now it became the practice of the Habibiyyin Darqawa to sing some *qasa'id* at any gathering in which they met, even if it was only to take tea. The Diwan has become so renowned and loved beyond the circle of the Darwaqa that it is now sung by Sufis all round the world. We have heard it sung in Makka, to the music of the *gamalang* from Indonesia, in Western America as well as in England."[188]

In addition to the Diwan of Muhammad ibn al-Habib, the *Nasiri Du'a* of the Moroccan Shaykh Muhammad ibn Nasir ad-Dar'i is used as a political tool in the Sufi *sama'* of the Habibiyya Darqawiyya order of 'Abdalqadir

187   Abdalqadir as-Sufi, *Root Islamic Education*, Ch. 1. On-line at http://bewley. virtualave.net viewed July 2007

188   Abdalqadir as-Sufi, "Preface to the Diwan of Shaykh Ibn al-Habib", *The Diwan of Shaykh Ibn al-Habib*, Madinah Press op. cit.

2. Chapter Two: Moroccan Influence in Britain

as-Sufi who instructed his followers to translate this *du'a* into English. The translation was done by the American Muslim scholar Aisha Bewley for the publishing house of the Habibiyya order, Madinah Press. It says in the introduction: "The Publication of this great *du'a* known as 'The sword of Ibn Nasir' has been undertake in response to the desire of Shaykh Abdalqadir as-Sufi that its collective recitation should be revived once more across the Muslim Ummah as a proven means of calling upon Allah's Generosity, and overcoming the enemies of the Deen."[189]

The lyrical ode, *al-Burda*, by Imam Sharaf ad-Din al-Busiri also plays an important part in the Sufi *sama'* gatherings of the Habibiyya order in Britain, as well as in other Western countries. The scholar Marcia Hermansen says, "Among the ritual practices of this movement are *dhikr*, recitation of Qur'an, and reciting the *wird* of the Darqawi *tariqa* transmitted from Shaykh Muhammad ibn al-Habib. In addition, the *Qasida al-Burda* is recited in large gatherings."[190] To hear the *Burda* sung in the Moroccan way, simply go to the website of Shaykh Abdalqadir as-Sufi and you will hear western voices singing the *qasida*, but in a clear Moroccan style, to the extent that you might imagine it to be the site of one of the internal Moroccan orders.

C. Literature and output

The arena of literary output is one of the main areas in which the beauty of Sufism manifests itself in the finest and most radiant way and the participation in this field of the Sufis of Morocco, despite its small size, is well-established and voluminous. Its influence has extended not only to Arab Muslims throughout the Muslim world, but also to areas of the Western world, far removed from it in cultural and social terms. This is a significant area in which the Moroccan presence has been manifested in Britain by the Habibiyya Darqawiyya, firstly through the translation of Moroccan Sufi texts into English and secondly by the preference shown by the shaykh and his followers for these texts and their attempt to put them

---

[189] See the works of Aisha Beweley on: http//:www.angelfire.com/ab/2bookwork/index.html

[190] Marcia Hermansen, "The 'Other' Shadhilis of the West" in *The Shadhiliyya*, op. cit., p.486

into practice. Although the second point still requires deeper study, in order for the different facets of this influence to be properly ascertained, the first point is evident since the Western Habibiyya order has certainly translated and published some collections of poetry and Sufi letters.

The translation and publication of the Diwan of Muhammad ibn al-Habib ad-Darqawi in several editions is an established fact, as is the translation of the letters of Shaykh 'Ali al-'Imrani al-Fasi, known as al-Jamal, which were published under the philosophical title: *The Meaning of Man*.[191] The letters of Shaykh al-'Arabi ad-Darqawi have also been translated into English and published under the title of *The Darqawi Way*.[192] In 2005 *The Collected Works of Ian Dallas* was published, consisting of three plays and four prose works.[193] A profound study of these works would be required to show how a Moroccan literary presence can be felt in them although I can definitely state now that it is clearly the case.

TOPIC TWO
THE MOROCCAN INFLUENCE ON THE *FIQH*, THEOLOGY AND POLITICS OF THE HABIBIYYA ORDER

1. MALIKI *FIQH*

A. The special quality of the Moroccan madhhab

One of the most notable manifestations of Moroccan influence on the Habibiyya order and its Shaykh Abdalqadir as-Sufi is their adoption of the Maliki school in *fiqh*. The Maliki school has spread in different areas of the world although the Moroccans are historically the nation with the longest adherence to it since they learned of it in the time of the Idrisid dynasty and it was confirmed later as the definitive national *madhhab* during the time of the Murabitun. All subsequent dynasties after that

---

191 'Ali al-Jamal al-'Amrani, *The Meaning of Man: The Foundations of the Science of Knowledge*, translated by: Aisha 'Abd ar-Rahman at-Tarjumana from the original text edited by: 'Abd al-Kabir al-Munawwara, Diwan Press, England (1977)

192 The letters of Shaykh al-'Arabi Darqawi have already been translated by Titus Burckhardt with the introduction of Martin Lings.

193 Ian Dallas, *Collected Works*, Budgate Press, Cape Town, 2005

2. Chapter Two: Moroccan Influence in Britain

held to it without deviating, with the one exception, for a limited period, of the Muwahhid state with its different theological direction.

Morocco has produced a large number of outstanding scholars of Maliki *fiqh*, whose influence spread both east and south, since the Qarawiyyin University became a focal point for the study of this *fiqh* and its texts. Before the appearance of the *Mukhtasar* of Shaykh Khalil (d. 776), the *Mudawwana* of Sahnun, *an-Nawadir* by Ibn Abi Zayd al-Qayrawani (d. 387), *Kitab at-Tahdhib* by al-Barada'i (d. 373), the book of Ibn Yunus (d. 451), and *al-Wadiha* of Ibn Habib (d. 238) were the most prominent books in circulation in the Qarawiyyin and the madrasas connected to it. After the appearance of the *Mukhtasar*, however, and the admiration of the Moroccans for it, the *fuqaha'* tended to specialise in commenting and doing glosses on it rather than the other texts.

Maliki *fiqh* continues to dominate the Qarawiyyin mosque university as well as other Moroccan religious foundations. Shaykh Muhammad ibn al-Habib ad-Darqawi, the shaykh of 'Abdalqadir as-Sufi (Ian Dallas) was himself a scholar in Maliki *fiqh* since he taught at the Qasba an-Nuwar mosque in Fes using *al-Murshid al-mu'in*, the *Mukhtasar* of Khalil and the *Muwatta'* of Imam Malik, and he also taught the *Risala* of Ibn Abi Zayd al-Qayrawani in the Zaytuna mosque in Meknes. This had a profound effect on his Scottish student, Ian Dallas, who absorbed Maliki *fiqh* along with Junaydi/Darqawi/Habibi Sufism and the Ash'ari creed. That is what is accepted as the religious norm in Moroccan Islam and finds its clear expression in the *Murshid al-Mu'in 'ala ad-Daruri min 'Ilum ad-Deen* known as the *Matn Ibn 'Ashir*, which says in its introductory verses:

Then, I ask for help from Allah, the Glorious
    in composing verses which will benefit the illiterate
In the Ash'ari creed and Malik *fiqh*
    and in the path of Sufism of Junayd.

As one of his followers says: "Thus Shaykh Abdalqadir entered Islam in Morocco and so his first acquaintance with the *fiqh* of Islam had automatically been by way of the Maliki *madhhab*"[194] and 'Abdalqadir as-Sufi himself explains this choice in his book, *Root Islamic Education* in

---

194 Abdalhaqq Bewley, "The Recovery of True Islamic Fiqh: An introduction to the work of Shaykh Abdalqadir as-Sufi" op. cit.

which he says: "Then, secondly, we come to the politics, law and hadith. For this we will take one book, which contains hadith, *usul* and the *'amal* of Madina, and that is *al-Muwatta'* of Imam Malik. *Al-Muwatta'* of Imam Malik is the earliest of our great books, of which Imam Shafi'i said: 'If there were any book after the Book of Allah by which I would swear, it would be *al-Muwatta'* of Imam Malik.'"[195]

B. The school of the practice (*'amal*) of the people of Madina

However the choice made by 'Abdalqadir as-Sufi to adopt this *fiqh* as a legal modality for his followers, indeed as a path to restore the situation of the Muslim nation as a whole, also had a logic behind it which leads to examining the true reasons why his inspired shaykhs among the Moroccan Sufis who preceded him preferred this school of *fiqh*. 'Abdalhaqq Bewley (one of his prominent followers) says in an essay of his in English, "The Recovery of True Islamic Fiqh, An Introduction to the work of Shaykh Abdalqadir as-Sufi": "His rediscovery of Imam Malik was, therefore, not as the founder of the subsequent *madhhab* named after him but rather as the Imam of the Dar al-Hijra, Madina al-Munawwara, and the recorder and transmitter of the *'Amal Ahli'l-Madina*, the practice of the people of Madina. Imam Malik saw it as his task to capture for posterity the living tradition of Islam in action, the Book and Sunna in their pristine original form, which had been passed down to him unaltered through the two generations that had elapsed since the Prophet's death, may Allah bless him and grant him peace."[196]

The soundness and purity of the school of Malik and its central source, based on the living practice of the people of Madina, is superior for two paramount reasons: "The first was that it clearly did represent the closest possible exposition of Islam as it was actually lived by the Prophet and his Companions. It constituted without any doubt the unbroken transmission of the Book and Sunna in the very place where it had been established, preserved and unaltered in any way by the two generations

---

195   Abdalqadir as-Sufi, *Root Islamic Education* Ch. 1. On line at http://bewley.virtualave.net viewed July 2007.

196   Abdalhaqq Bewley, "The Recovery of True Islamic Fiqh: An introduction to the work of Shaykh Abdalqadir as-Sufi" op. cit.

2. Chapter Two: Moroccan Influence in Britain

who had lived there between the days of the First Community and the time of Imam Malik. So what it brings to us is that raw, vital energy of the first days of Islam, the time of the Prophet himself, may Allah bless him and grant him peace, and the time immediately following it of the Khulafa Rashidun, may Allah be pleased with all of them, when the deen was in its most potent phase of expansion and establishment. For that reason it is sometimes known as the *madhhab* of 'Umar, may Allah be pleased with him...."

"The second reason is its incontrovertible authenticity which has been repeatedly verified throughout the centuries, not least by the celebrated Hanbali scholar, Ibn Taymiyya, whose book *The Soundness of the Basic Premises of the Madhhab of the People of Madina*, makes it clear that the most complete picture of the Sunna, both in terms of its spirit and its actual practice, was that passed on by Imam Malik and captured in its outline in his book *al-Muwatta'*. This was because of Imam Malik's great knowledge, his geographical location in the City of the Prophet, the great number of men of knowledge who had remained there, preserving the deen in its entirety from the time of the Prophet, may Allah bless him and grant him peace, and the fact that, as was universally acknowledged, no innovation in the deen at all entered Madina during the first three generations of Islam."[197]

This pure deen is to be found among the Moroccans, rather than Muslims in the East, because of the transmission of the pure Islamic Maliki school to the West, as Shaykh Abdalqadir as-Sufi says, "In North Africa, and this is very important because the teaching went west. What you have to understand is that the main body of Islam, the Islam that we have been talking about, did not go east to Nishapur, it did not go north to Iraq. It went west. Islam went to Africa. This is the historical fact that was obliterated by the power-structure which followed."[198]

---

197 Abdalhaqq Bewley, "The Recovery of True Islamic Fiqh: An introduction to the work of Shaykh Abdalqadir as-Sufi", op. cit.

198 Abdalqadir As-Sufi, *Root Islamic Education*, Summary – Part One, on line at http://bewley.virtualave.net viewed July 2007

2. POLITICAL REFORM

A. The Murabitun state as a model

This conviction of upholding the school of Malik as a firm basis for rectifying the course of the Islamic nation and reviving its deen required a political programme through which the desire of Shaykh Abdalqadir as-Sufi to see this come about might be realised, based on a glorious precedent within the history of Islam. In this context Shaykh Abdalqadir as-Sufi, using the Moroccan legacy, drew up a directive programme, showing how the school of Malik was able to usher in, on at least one occasion, days of glory for the Muslim nation, referring to the political programme of the Murabitun state. Abdalhaqq Bewley says: "The historical proof of its (the *madhhab's*) potency can be seen in the example of the Murabitun in the eleventh century. The Practice of the People of Madina was transmitted to them by Abdallah ibn Yasin, the teacher sent to them from Kairouan, where the living record of the *'Amal Ahli'l-Madina* had been passed on from the time of Malik himself, and with it and nothing else they burst out from their land in West Africa and revived Islam throughout the Maghrib and al-Andalus, ensuring the Muslims in Spain, who had at that time almost come under Christian domination, a further two hundred years of Islamic governance."[199]

It is known that the appearance of the Murabitun and the secret of their strength derived from a group of factors which Professor Abbas al-Jarari condenses to three and says: "The third, and it is important, is the reliance of the Murabitun, in the principles of their reforming movement, on the Maliki school. The Moroccans were ready to accept these principles since they were already known for the school which was in harmony with their nature."[200]

So the Shaykh of the Habibiyya order in the West changed the name of his order from the Habibiyya Darqawiyya to the Worldwide Murabitun Movement, aiming to restore the situation of the Muslim nation by

[199] Abdalhaqq Bewley, "The Recovery of True Islamic Fiqh: An introduction to the work of Shaykh Abdalqadir as-Sufi", op. cit.

[200] Al-Jirari, 'Abbas, *"al-Adab al-Maghribi min khilal Dhawahirihi wa Qadayah"*. Library of Ma'aref for print and publication. Ch.1, Vol.3, (1986CE/1406AH) p.87

2. Chapter Two: Moroccan Influence in Britain

following a new reforming political programme based on the practice of the people of Madina, the purity of the Maliki school, and its openness and receptivity to serious new efforts to see it re-established. Any political reform, however, if it is go beyond theory and into real implementation, must have capable individuals who are able to take on responsibility for it and fulfil its promises of rule and justice.

B. The personality of the judge: Qadi 'Iyad as a model

So once more we find Shaykh Abdalqadir as-Sufi examining Moroccan history to elicit a model for his religious and political programme in the form of an exemplary man, a man combining legal judgment, since he was a Qadi who was able to authorise "cutting heads, and hands, and marking backs, and passing sentences, and giving orders to Amirs,"[201] with scrupulousness, religious asceticism, love for the Messenger of Allah ﷺ, and exemplary scholarship, since he was one the most notable scholars of the age. This man was Qadi 'Ayad ibn Musa al-Yahsubi.

It was necessary for Shaykh Abdalqadir as-Sufi to begin by acquainting his followers with this man and his deeds. So he set out to translate his books, especially *ash-Shifa*, which is the third in his order of texts after the Noble Qur'an and the *Muwatta'* of Imam Malik. Abdalhaqq Bewley says: "Shaykh Abdalqadir had already been responsible for the first complete English translation of Malik's great book, *al-Muwatta'*, but now he saw it with new eyes as the blueprint for the re-establishment of Allah's deen in the very same way in which it had been established in the first place. Put together with Allah's Book and the *Shifa'* of Qadi 'Iyad, which provides the essential inner dimension of love of the Messenger, it is all that is necessary for the complete re-implementation of Islamic governance."[202] Who was Qadi 'Iyad? And why specifically was Qadi 'Iyad chosen?

Qadi 'Iyad was one of the most prominent scholars of Morocco in the knowledges of the Shari'a, especially the *fiqh* of Malik. It is said about him: "Were it not for Qadi 'Iyad, the Maghrib would not have been known."

---

201 Abdalqadir as-Sufi, *Root Islamic Education*, Ch.1, on line at http://bewley.virtualave.net viewed July 2007

202 Abdalhaqq Bewley, "The Recovery of True Islamic Fiqh: An introduction to the work of Shaykh Abdalqadir as-Sufi", op. cit.

That is an assessment of his major role in laying out a new foundation for the scholars of Morocco, who were previously suspected of merely imitating those in the east. 'Iyad on the other hand surpassed the scholars of the east in knowledge and became someone to whom people travelled. His books covered different spheres of knowledge and scholars vied with one another in memorising them and using them for evidence. The Sufis continue to teach them and to encourage their *murids* to take from them, especially *ash-Shifa bi-ta'rif huquq al-Mustafa* which Shaykh Abdalqadir became aware of inside the Habibiyya order where it had been taught by Shaykh ibn al-Habib in the Zaytuna Mosque in Meknes.

That is why Madina Press, which is connected to the order of Abdalqadir as-Sufi, worked to publish the English translation of *ash-Shifa* under the title: *Muhammad: the Messenger of Allah*, and another book of 'Iyad published by the same press under the title *The Foundations of Islam*. It is a small book, divided into five parts, each one concerning one of the five pillars of Islam. The book deals with each of the five pillars giving the details of its rulings: *fard*, sunna, recommended, disliked and forbidden. It is a useful book for new Muslims, but it also refreshes the knowledge of educated scholars.[203] The books of Qadi 'Iyad are a constant source of reference for Shaykh Abdalqadir as-Sufi and his followers, borne out by the fact that he quotes from him in most of his books and they are also used as evidence by followers of the Shaykh in their essays, books and lectures. Nevertheless the question which poses itself is: Why Qadi 'Iyad in particular?

The answer can be summarised simply under five headings:

1. Qadi 'Iyad held to the Maliki school. Indeed, he participated in preserving it, defining it and spreading it. It was he who organised the *Mudawwana* of Sahnun, which is indisputably one of the primary sources of Maliki *fiqh*, into chapters. Many commentaries, summaries and glosses had been written on the *Mudawwana*. However, before him, it did not have proper chapters, so that different questions were muddled together, and due to the lack of precision it was difficult to connect traditions with the legal questions relating to them. So Qadi 'Iyad undertook to

---

203   http://www.shaykhabdalqadir.com/content/books.html

edit its transmissions, name its transmitters, explain its difficult words and set it in order. That was in his book, *at-Tanbihat al-mustabata 'ala al-kutub al-mudawaana wa'l-mukhtalata*. There is no doubt that Qadi 'Iyad's undertaking of this work was an important step on the path of defining the Maliki school and making it flourish.

2. His defence of the practice of the people of Madina in his book *Tartib al-Madarik* clarifies the excellence of the knowledge of the people of Madina and defends the theory of the Malikis in adopting the practice of the people of Madina as one of the principles of legislation which the school relies on.

3. He combines *fiqh* and tasawwuf in his books and his book, *ash-Shifa*, provides the best evidence of that. All of it deals with aspects of the Muhammadan nature, the path of truth, and deals with the *sira* of the Prophet ﷺ which is filled with miracles and indications to incite the soul to spiritual advancement.

4. One of the prominent aspects of the Murabitun dynasty, which Abdalqadir as-Sufi has worked to revive, is the call based on devotional practice and holding to Maliki *fiqh* while trying to enhance it by adding Sufism to it, and this was perfectly exemplified in 'Iyad's life.

5. 'Iyad embodied the characteristics of a just judge and a resolute political reformer, ruled by a clear vision of the deen and *madhhab*, accompanied by a strong religious practice and great love for the Messenger of Allah ﷺ, and these are the very characteristics encouraged in the political project which the western Habibiyya Darqawiyya order seeks to realise.

3. THE ASH'ARI CREED

A. The special quality of the Moroccan creed

In their holding to the Ash'ari creed, the Habibiyya Darqawiyya order and its Shaykh Abdalqadir as-Sufi also follow the Moroccan tradition, especially that of the shaykhs of Sufism who encouraged combining the Sufi path and the Maliki school in *fiqh* with the adoption of the Ash'ari creed. That is because the views of the Malikis and the Ash'aris are very similar. The adoption of the Maliki school by the Moroccans gave strong support to the creed of the people of the Sunna, because Imam Malik's position with respect to theology and creed opposed the positions of the deviant schools and had a similar basis to that of the Ash'aris and their school. That is why the Maliki *madhhab* and the Ash'ari creed go together and are combined with the Sufism of al-Junayd. That is how creed, *fiqh* and Sufism are linked together in Moroccan thought.

There are two main reasons for the adoption of the Ash'ari creed by the Moroccans. Firstly the connection between the Maliki Moroccans and the Ash'ari thinkers in the east was brought about by a number of great thinkers in al-Andalus, Morocco and Tunis who studied in the East and learned their legal and creedal studies from the great Ash'aris there. When they returned to their countries, they returned completely convinced by this school and the necessity of spreading it and making it common among the people there.

2. Moroccans believe that the Ash'ari creed is the 'saved sect' transmitted in the well-known prophetic hadith.[204] The creed of the Moroccans is the Ash'arite creed because: "the Ash'arite creed is distinguished by being comprehensive, median, and successful. Scholars have confirmed the great efforts which Abu al-Hasan al-Ash'ari went to in order to restore the Salafi Sunni creed to its sound original foundations and pure belief. They all agreed that the Ash'arite creed is the creed of the people of the Sunna and Community," and that has continued to be the case down to the present time. Ash'arite thought in the Islamic west in general, and in Morocco in particular, is a balanced version of the school, purely based on the position of its founder, Abu al-Hasan al-Ash'ari. It has not been affected by more extreme Ash'arite offshoots in the east, such as those of Juwayni and Baqillani.[205]

B. The *kalam* position of the western Habibiyya order

That is why Shaykh Abdalqadir as-Sufi chose the Ash'arite creed in particular, and the exposition of al-Ghazali in the science of *kalam*. He says: "The Ghazali position became a dominant factor. It was not

---

204 It is a well known Prophetic hadith (saying).

205 http//:www.islam-maroc.gov.ma/ar/detail.aspx?id&1619=z&14=s1=

2. Chapter Two: Moroccan Influence in Britain

particularly in relation to the sufic phenomenon, but it was Imam al-Ghazali in his role as the one who presented a view of *kalam*, of the 'how-you-talk-about' Allah, *subhanahu wa ta'ala,* and what is now known as the Ash'ari position. The Ash'ari *kalam* talks about Allah, *subhanahu wa ta'ala*, in terms of necessary attributes, the mother attributes, the acts of Allah, the attributes of Allah, and the essence of Allah, and so on and so on ... and latter is the formula which becomes popularised right down to the time of Ibn 'Ashir where he divides the deen into the *kalam* of Ash'ari, the *fiqh* of Malik, and the tasawwuf of Imam Junayd."[206]

So this Moroccan influence can be seen in the western Habibiyya Darqawiyya order, which has spread from its centre in Britain to all parts of the world, and it has clearly been shown, without any room for doubt, that Morocco has the capacity to provide a religious model which can be emulated anywhere in the world. It can be propagated by means of Sufism and provide light for a dialogue with the West and a means of convincing them of the benefit of Islamic spiritual practice.

---

[206] Abdalqadir as-Sufi, *Root Islamic Education*, "Summary – Part One: 'Amal", on line at: http://bewley.virtualave.net viewed July 2007

CONCLUSION

THIS BOOK HAS attempted to study the appearance of the phenomenon of Islamic Sufism in the West, which first began by adopting a universalist philosophical form with the Universalist order of Inayat Khan. The goal of that was to be in keeping with the intellectual and political landscape prevalent in the West in the twentieth century, which used to see Sufism as disconnected from the Islamic religion. This view quickly came into conflict with the reality of Muslim Sufism which appeared with the foundation of the western branches of the Darqawiyya Shadhiliya. The scholar Mark Sedgwick says: "During the twentieth century the view of Sufism as something separate from Islam became widespread in the West, but it is essential to appreciate that this view is a purely Western one ... In Algeria and elsewhere in the Islamic world, Islam and Sufism were and are inseparable. Sufis are by definition Muslim, and the religious practices of a Sufi are based on the careful observance of the Sharia."[207] Sufism is the spiritual path inside Islam and if we separate it from this understanding, it becomes something very different indeed.[208]

The western Shadhiliyya *tariqas* and their different branches took on a leading role in changing the understanding of Sufi thought prevailing in the West and directed it and gradually moved it towards its true Islamic basis, influenced by the profound Sufi experience existing in the Islamic world. The Western branch of the 'Alawiyya Darqawiyya branch was one of the first Muslim Sufi *tariqas* which was able to imprint its special qualities on the intellectual and philosophical arena in the West and

207 Mark Sedgwick, *Against the Modern World: Traditionalism and the Secret Intellectual History of the Twentieth Century* op. cit., p.65

208 Mark J. Sedgwick, *Le Sufisme*, Traduit de l'anglais par: Jean-François Mayer, Les Editions du Cerf, 2001, p.91

prepared the way for the appearance of other Muslim Sufi orders.

One of the most conspicuous of these is the western branch of the Habibiyya Darqawiyya order which originated in Morocco and brought to the West, particularly the Anglo-Saxon world, the Moroccan form of Sufism which is based on three elements: the path of al-Junayd in Sufism, the Maliki school in *fiqh* – based on the practice of the people of Madina – and the Ash'arite creed in theology – to which the people of the Sunna and Community hold.

These three particularly Moroccan religious characteristics, which are prominent in the order, represent a lighthouse of openness, tolerance and ability to relate to other peoples. They also make it a very supple order, which is able to adapt to different environments and at the same time break through the barriers and restrictions of time and place, even Western ones. Just a brief glance at the Moroccan texts translated into English by the publishing house of the Habibiyya order shows the strength of the profound influence which Moroccan Sufism has had and continues to have within the order.

APPENDICES

1. ARABIC COPY OF LETTER OF SHAYKH 'ADDA BEN TUNIS

بسم الله الرحمن الرحيم

الحمد لله وكفى وسلام على عباده الذين اصطفى

اما بعد يا اخي اشهد والله خبي الشاهد بين شيما ان خالصة لوده
اليكم انه قد عدنا هنا ذو الشعبين الكريم والاخلاق الطيبة نصوع
التودة الم بي ان الله حبيبى حبيبى نورالدين ورباوى دا واولادنا
انه قد عدنا هنا العمد الغريب معاشرة مديدة يمكن معها عدة برة
احوال الحي وانواله وعياله وما رايته منه وانموز بغاية الاهما يظهر
للمؤمن وبذلة المنتسب الخالصة الطبيعة الجميلى الاذى يجتنبى الابتم
من يشاء ، ويبعدى البم من يشيب .

ولنشاء على ما نقدم من موجى ... الله في ليل الله فى الذى هداه الله
على لسانى المحمدية الاسلامية جبهة بيت اجراد غموض من الوريانيا
من نلفى كلمة التوحيد د لااله الاالله محمد رسول الله ، وما
ينبعثها من الواجبات الدينية غفار تعالى د وصى عسى فولارحمن
د عبادى الله وجعل عظم وفى إننى من المسلمين ، وانى اوصيه
ولنفسى بتقوى الله في السر والنجوى وإن يجتنب مطامع
النعيس عن ابتاح السهو وإن يتوكل على الله في جميع شؤوده
د وصى يتوكل على الله يهو حسبه إن الله بالغ امره قد جعل الله لكل
شيء قدرا :

حرره عبد ربه الفانى لامر الرا حى حبيبك بمكة وفضله
الواضع خطه بيده

2. CHART OF THE NAMES OF THE MAIN SUFIS MENTIONED

Original Name	Muslim Name	Original Country
Ian Dallas	Abdalqadir as-Sufi al-Murabit	Scotland
Ivan Aguili	Mustafa Aguili	Sweden
Alphonse-Etienne Dinet	Nasr ad-Din	France
Isabelle Iberhardt	Isabelle	Russia
Bewley	Abdalhaqq Bewley	England
Bewley's Wife	Aisha Abdurrahman at-Tarjumana	USA
Titus Burkhardt	Ibrahim 'Izz ad-Din	Switzerland
Durkee	Abdullah Nur ad-Din	USA
Durkee's wife	Al-Hajja Nura	USA
Renee Guénon	Abdalwahid Yahya	France
Inayat Khan	Hazrat Inayat Khan	India
Frithjof Schuon	Isa Nur ad-Din	Switzerland
Martin Lings	Abu Bakr Siraj ad-Din	England
Mark Hansen	Hamza Yusuf	USA
Michal Valsan	Shaykh Mustafa	Romania
Nuh Ha Mim Keller	Shaykh Nuh Ha Mim	USA

Appendices

3. CHART OF MOROCCAN TEXTS TRANSLATED AND PUBLISHED BY THE HABIBIYYA

Subject	Publisher	Translator
Tasawwuf: *Sufis and Sufism: A Defence,* English translation of *Kitab al-Huwar*, a treatise by the Moroccan Shaykhs 'Abdalhaqq al-'Amrawi and 'Abdalkarim Murad (both formerly shaykhs in the Qarawiyyin mosque in Fes) defending Tasawwuf and Sufism against the attacks of Wahhabis and Salafis	Madinah Press, 2004	– Aisha and Abdalhaqq Bewley – Introduction by Shaykh Abdalqadir as-Sufi
Tasawwuf: translation of the Diwan *Bughyat al-Murideen as-Sa'ireen wa Tuhfat as-Salikeen al-'Arifeen* by Muhammad ibn al-Habib ad-Darqawi	Madinah Press	– Aisha and Abdalhaqq Bewley – Introduction by Shaykh Abdalqadir as-Sufi
Tasawwuf. *The Basic Research*, translation of *Al-Futuhatul Ilahiyya fi Sharh Al-Mabahith Al-Asliyya* by Shaykh Ahmad ibn 'Ajiba	Madinah Press	– Aisha Abdarrahman Bewley
Tasawwuf: *The Darqawi Way*, an English translation of the collected letters of Shaykh al-'Arabi ad-Darqawi sent to his murids	Diwan Press, 1979	– Aisha Abdarrahman Bewley

Tasawwuf: *The Two Invocations*, a translation of the book of Shaykh Mustafa al-'Alawi on the subject of the Unique Name and on the *du'a 'Kanz al-Haqa'iq'* by Shaykh Muhamad ibn al-Habib ad-Darqawi	Madina Press	— Aisha Abdarrahman Bewley — Abdassamad Clarke
Tasawwuf: *The Nasiri Du'a*, the translation of the *du'a* of the Morroccan Shaykh Muhammad ibn Nasir ad-Dari'i known as "The Sword of Ibn Nasir". This book was printed in an Arabic/English edition at the request of Shaykh Abdalqadir as-Sufi	Madinah Press	— Aisha Abdarrahman Bewley
Sira of the Prophet ﷺ: *Muhammad, Messenger of Allah*, the translation of the book *ash-Shifa* by the Moroccan *'alim* buried in Marrakesh, Qadi 'Iyad	Madinah Press, 1991	— Aisha Abdarrahman and Abdalhaqq Bewley
Maliki fiqh: *The Foundations of Islam*, a translation of the book *Qawa'id al-Islam*, according to the practice of the people of Madina by the Moroccan Maliki faqih, Qadi 'Iyad	Madinah Press	— Aisha Abdarrahman and Abdalhaqq Bewley

Tasawwuf: *The Meaning of Man,* translation of a collection of letters, directions and counsels from Shaykh 'Ali al-'Imrani, known as al-Jamal	Diwan Pess, 1977	– Aisha Abdarrahman Bewley – Introduction by Shaykh Abdalqadir as-Sufi
Fiqh: *Defence Against Disaster* translation of *Al-'Awasim min al-Qawasim* by Moroccan Malik faqih, Abu Bakr Muhammad ibn 'Abdullah ibn al-'Arabi al-Ma'afiri, who is buried in Fez	Madinah Press, 1996	– Aisha Abdarrahman Bewley

ISLAMIC SUFISM IN THE WEST

4. CHART OF SILSILA OF SHAYKH ABDALQADIR

In the Name of Allah the Merciful the Compassionate

Sayyiduna
Muhammad
blessings and peace of Allah be upon him

Sayyiduna 'Ali ibn Abi Talib

Sayyidi al-Hasan ibn 'Ali Sayyidi Abu Muhammad Jabir Sayyidi Sa'id al-Gharwani Sayyidi Fatha's-Su'ud Sayyidi Sa'd Sayyidi Sa'id Sayyidi Ahmad al-Marwani Sayyidi Ibrahim al-Basri Sayyidi Zaynu'd-Din al-Qazwini Sayyidi Muhammad Shamsu'd-Din Sayyidi Muhammad Taju'd-Din Sayyidi Nuru'd-Din Abu'l-Hasan 'Ali Sayyidi Fakhuru'd-Din Sayyidi Tuqayyu'd-Din Sayyidi 'Abd'ar-Rahman al-'Attar	**In the Name of Allah, the Merciful, the Compassionate.** **Say: 'He is Allah, One. Allah, as-Samad. He has not begotten, nor was he begotten, and no-one is like Him.'**	Sayyidi al-Hasan al-Basri Sayyidi Habib al-'Ajami Sayyidi Da'ud at-Ta'i Sayyidi Ma'ruf al-Karkhi Sayyidi as-Sari as-Saqti Al-Imam al-Junayd Sayyidi ash-Shibli Sayyidi at-Tartusi Sayyidi Abu'l-Hasan al-Hakkari Sayyidi Abu Sai'id al-Mubarak Mawlana 'Abdal-Qadir al-Jilani Sayyidi Abu Madyan al-Ghawth Sayyidi Muhammad Salih Sayyidi Muhammad ibn Harazim

Sayyidi 'Abdu's-Salam ibn Mashish
Sayyidi Abu'l-Hasan ash-Shadhili
Sayyidi Abu'l-Abbas al-Mursi
Sayyidi Ahmad ibn 'Ata'Illah
Sayyidi Da'ud al-Bakhili
Sayyidi Muhammad Wafa
Sayyidi 'Ali Wafa
Sayyidi Yahya al-Qadiri
Sayyidi Ahmad al-Hadrami
Sayyidi Ahmad az-Zarruq
Sayyidi Ibrahim al-Fahham
Sayyidi 'Ali ad-Dawwar
Sayyidi 'Abd'ar-Rahman al-Majdhub
Sayyidi Yusuf al-Fasi
Sayyidi 'Abdu'r-Rahman al-Fasi
Sayyidi Muhammad ibn 'Abdillah
Sayyidi Qasim al-Khassasi
Sayyidi Ahmad ibn 'Abdillah
Sayyidi al-'Arabi ibn 'Abdillah
Sayyidi 'Ali al-Jamal
Mawlay al-'Arabi ibn Ahmad ad-Darqawi

**The Chain of Teachers
of the Shadhiliyya
– Darqawiyya – Habibiyya
Tariqa
from their source,
may the blessings
and peace of Allah
be upon him,
up to the present day.**

Sayyidi Abu Ya'za al-Mahaji Sayyidi Muhammad ibn 'Abd'al-Qadir al-Basha Sayyidi Muhammad ibn Qadur Sayyidi ibn al-Habib al-Buzidi Mawlana Ahmad ibn Mustafa al-'Alawi Sayyidi Muhammad al-Fayturi Hamuda	**And there came from the farthest part of the city a man running. He said, 'O my people, follow those who have been sent.'**	Sayyidi Ahmad al-Badawi Sayyidi Muhammad al-'Arabi Sayyidi al-'Arabi al-Hawsari Sayyidi Muhammad ibn 'Ali Sayyidi Muhammad ibn al-Habib

Sayyidi 'Abd al-Qadir as-Sufi ad-Darqawi al-Murabit

Appendices

5. CHART OF SILSILA OF INAYAT KHAN

سلسلة الوراثة الروحية الإسلامية لحضرة عنايات خان [1]

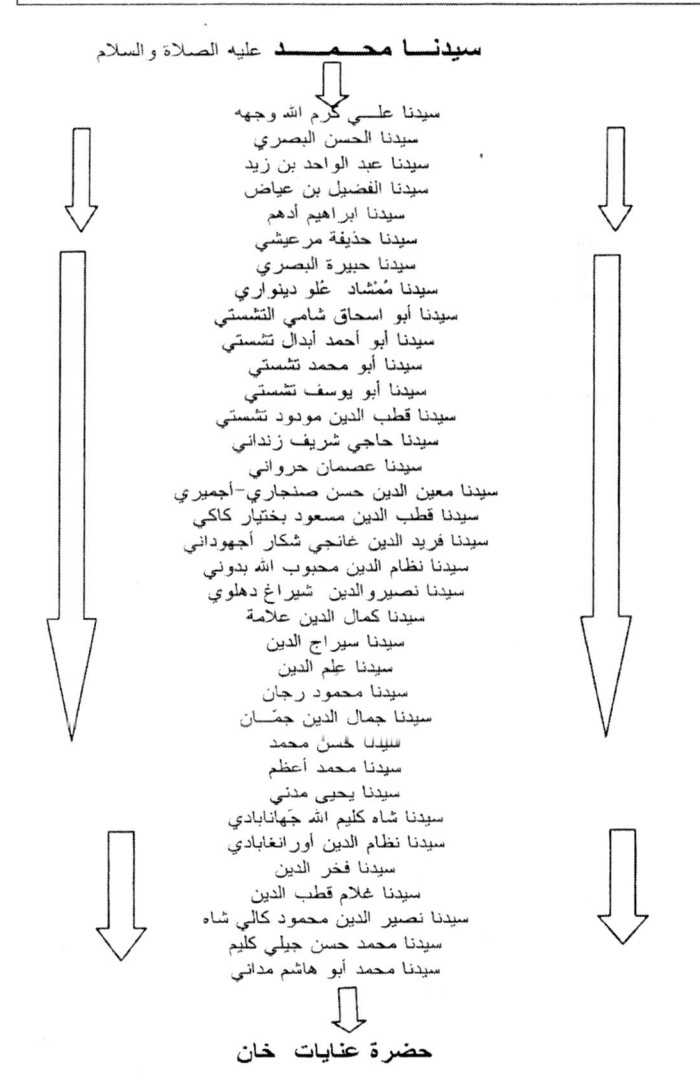

سيدنا محمد عليه الصلاة والسلام

سيدنا علي كرم الله وجهه
سيدنا الحسن البصري
سيدنا عبد الواحد بن زيد
سيدنا الفضيل بن عياض
سيدنا ابراهيم أدهم
سيدنا حذيفة مرعيشي
سيدنا حبيرة البصري
سيدنا مُمْشاد عُلو دينواري
سيدنا أبو اسحاق شامي التشستي
سيدنا أبو أحمد أبدال تشستي
سيدنا أبو محمد تشستي
سيدنا أبو يوسف تشستي
سيدنا قطب الدين مودود تشستي
سيدنا حاجي شريف زنداني
سيدنا عصمان حرواني
سيدنا معين الدين حسن صنجاري-أجميري
سيدنا قطب الدين مسعود بختيار كاكي
سيدنا فريد الدين غانجي شكار أجهودواني
سيدنا نظام الدين محبوب الله بدوني
سيدنا نصيروالدين شيراغ دهلوي
سيدنا كمال الدين علامة
سيدنا سيراج الدين
سيدنا علم الدين
سيدنا محمود رجان
سيدنا جمال الدين جمّان
سيدنا حسن محمد
سيدنا محمد أعظم
سيدنا يحيى مدني
سيدنا شاه كليم الله جهانابادي
سيدنا نظام الدين أورانغابادي
سيدنا فخر الدين
سيدنا غلام قطب الدين
سيدنا نصير الدين محمود كالي شاه
سيدنا محمد حسن جيلي كليم
سيدنا محمد أبو هاشم مدني

حضرة عنايات خان

ALLAH
Hazrat Jlbra'il
Hazrat Khwaja Muhammad Rasul Allah
Hazrat Khwaja 'Ali Wali Allah
Hazrat Khwaja Hasan Basri
Hazrat Khwaja 'Abd al-Wahid bin Zayd
Hazrat Khwaja Fuzayl bin 'Iyaz
Hazrat Khwaja Ibrahim Adham
Hazrat Khwaja Huzayfa Mar'ishi
Hazrat Khwaja Hubayra Basri
Hazrat Khwaja Mumshad 'Ulu Dinwari
Hazrat Khwaja Abu Ishaq Shami
Hazrat Khwaja Abu Ahmad Abdal Chishti
Hazrat Khwaja Abu Muhammad Chishti
Hazrat Khwaja Abu Yusuf Chishti
Hazrat Khwaja Qutbuddin Mawdud Chishti
Hazrat Khwaja Hajji Sharif Zindani
Hazrat Khwaja 'Usman Harvani
Hazrat Khwaja Mu'inuddin Hasan Sanjari-Ajmiri
Hazrat Khwaja Qutbuddin Mas'ud Bakhtiyar Kaki
Hazrat Khwaja Fariduddin Ganj-i Shakar Ajhodani
Hazrat Khwaja Nizamuddin Mahbub-i Llahi Badauni
Hazrat Khwaja Nasiruddin Chiragh Dihlavi
Hazrat Shaykh al-Masha'ikh Kamaluddin 'Allama
Hazrat Shaykh al-Masha'ikh Sirajuddin
Hazrat Shaykh al-Masha'ikh 'Ilmuddin
Hazrat Shaykh al-Masha'ikh Mahmud Rajan
Hazrat Shaykh al-Masha'ikh Jamaluddin Jamman
Hazrat Shaykh al-Masha'ikh Hasan Muhammad
Hazrat Shaykh al-Masha'ikh Muhammad A'zam
Hazrat Shaykh al-Masha'ikh Yahya Madani
Hazrat Shaykh al-Masha'ikh Shah Kalim Allah Jahanabadi
Hazrat Shaykh al-Masha'ikh Nizamuddin Awrangabadi
Hazrat Shaykh al-Masha'ikh Maulana Fakhruddin
Hazrat Shaykh al-Masha'ikh Ghulam Qutbuddin
Hazrat Shaykh al-Masha'ikh Nasiruddin Mahmud Kali Shah
Hazrat Shaykh al-Masha'ikh Muhammad Hasan Jili Kalimi
Hazrat Shaykh al-Masha'ikh Abu Hashim Madani
Hazrat Pir-o-Murshid Inayat Khan

Bibliography

I. ARABIC BIBLIOGRAPHY

– القرآن الكريم برواية ورش.
* The Noble Qur'an: Warsh Recitation.

* أحمد القطعاني، حراس العقيدة، مكتبة مكناس للطبع والتوزيع – طرابلس، ليبيا – ط.٢ سنة:٢٠٠١م/١٤٢٢هـ.
* Al-Qat'ani, Ahmad. *Hurras al-'aqida*. Library of Méknes for Print and Publication.Tripoli: Libya.Second edition (2001 CE/1422AH).

* ريتشارد سوذرن، صورة الإسلام في أوروبا في القرون الوسطى، ترجمة: د. رضوان السيد– دار المدار الإسلامي الطبعة٢ سنة:٢٠٠٦.
* Southern, Richard. *Surat al-Islam fi Uruppa fi'l-Qurun al-Wusta*. Translated by: Redwan Assayyed. House of al-Madar al-Islami. 2nd edition (2006).

* صلاح عبد الرزاق "الإسلام الأوروبي" – جريدة المدى – عدد:٩٦٧، اسم الصفحة: آراء وأفكار، تاريخ ١٠ يونيو ٢٠٠٧
* 'Abd Razzak, Salah. "Al-Islam al-Urubi" in: Journal of al-Mada, N. 967, (10 June, 2007).

* عباس الجراري، الأدب المغربي من خلال ظواهره وقضاياه، مكتبة المعارف للنشر والتوزيع، الجزء١، ط.٣، (١٤٠٦هـ/١٩٨٦م).
* Al-Jirari, 'Abbas. "Al-Adab al-Maghribi min khilal Dhawahirihi wa Qadayah". Library of Ma'aref for print and publication. Ch.1, Vol.3, (1986CE/1406AH).

* عبد الرحمان بدوي، دور العرب في تكوين الفكر الأوروبي – الطبعة ٣ سنة

- 119 -

١٩٧٩ منشورات وكالة المطبوعات – الكويت – ودار القلم – بيروت.

* Badawi, 'Abd Rahman. *Dawr al-'Arab fi Takwin al Fikr al-Urubi*. 3rd edition. Publications of Printing Agency, Kuwait and Dar al-Qalam, Beirut (1979).

* عبد السلام الغرميني، الصوفي والآخر: دراسات نقدية في الفكر الإسلامي المقارن، شركة النشر والتوزيع – المدارس– الدار البيضاء، ط١. (١٤٢١ه/٢٠٠٠م).

* Al-Gharmini, 'Abd-as-Salam. *As-Sufi Wal-Akhar*: Dirasat Naqdiyya fi al-Fikr al-Islami al-Muqarin. Al-Madaris for Print and Publication: Casablanca. 1st edition (2000CE/1421 AH).

* عبد الوهاب الفيلالي، الأدب الصوفي في المغرب إبان القرنين الثامن عشر والتاسع عشر للميلاد – ظواهر وقضايا – ، أطروحة لنيل دكتوراه الدولة في اللغة العربية وآدابها –تخصص أدب مغربي– جامعة سيدي محمد بن عبد الله، كلية الآداب والعلوم الإنسانية، ظهر المهراز بفاس، السنة الجامعية: ١٤٢١/١٤٢٢ه– ٢٠٠٠/٢٠٠١م، تحت إشراف: د.أحمد العراقي.

* El-Filali, 'Abdel-Wahhab. *Al-Adab as-Sufi fi'l-Maghrib Ibana Al-Qarnayn 18&19 CE: Dhawahir wa Qadaya*. A thesis submitted for the fulfillment of the requirement of a Doctorate in Philosophy in Arabic studies specialising in Moroccan Literature. Sidi Muhammad ibn Abdullah University Dhahr Mihraz – Fez. Under the supervision of Doctor Ahmad al-'Iraqi (2000-2001CE/1421-1422AH).

* عنايات خان، تعاليم المتصوفين، ترجمة: ابراهيم استنبولي، دار الفرقد ط١ سنة ٢٠٠٦م – دمشق، سوريا.

* Inayat Khan. *Ta'alim al-Mutasawwifin*, Translated by: Ibrahim Istanbuli. House of al-Farqad: Syria: Damascus, 1st edition (2006).

* فاروق نصر متولي وهبة العارف بالله: سيدي سلامة الراضي رضي الله عنه: الفيلسوف و الصوفي والشاعر والأديب الجزء الأول: الصوفي. ط١. سنة: ١٤٠٩ه/١٩٨٨م

* Nasr Mutawalli Wahba, Faruq. *Al-'Arif Billah: Sidi Salama ar-Radi: al-Faylasuf wa as-Sufi wa ash-Sha'ir wa al-Adib*, (1st Volume). 1st edition (1988CE/1409AH).

* فريثجوف شيوون الإيمان الإسلام والإحسان في مقارنة الأديان، ترجمة: نهاد خياطة، المؤسسة الجامعية للدراسات والنشر والتوزيع – بيروت- ط.١٩٩٦م /١٤١٦هـ.

* Schuon, Frithjof. *Al-Iman al-Islam Wa al-Ihsan Fi Muqaranati al-Adyan*, translated by: Nihad Khayyata, University Press for Studies, Print and Publication: Beirut. 1st edition (1996CE/1416AH).

* مجموعة من الباحثين: المعجم الفلسفي – مجمع اللغة العربية – عالم الكتب – بيروت – ١٩٧٩م/١٣٩٩هـ

* Many Researchers: *Philosophical Dictionary*. Arabic Language Academy, The World of Books: Beirut (1979CE/1399AH).

* محمد الخداري، "الدور السياسي للطريقة الدرقاوية في العلاقات بين المغرب والجزائر في بداية القرن التاسع عشر"-المناهل- الزوايا في المغرب الجزء الأول.

* Al-Khidari, Muhammad. "Ad-Dawr as-Siyasi li Tariqa ad-Darqawiya Fi al-'Alaqat bayna al-Maghrib Wa al-Jaza'ir fi Bidayat al-Qarn at-Tasi' 'Ashar" in: al-Manahil Magazine, Az-Zawaya Fi al-Maghrib Ch.1.

* محمد عصام عيدو "انطفأ سراج أبو بكر" مارتن لينغز" (١٩٠٩ – ٢٠٠٥م) نقلا عن الموقع الإلكتروني للملتقى الفكري:
http://www.almultaka.net/makalat.php?subaction=showfull&id=11 17481536&archive=&start_from=&ucat=3&

* 'Isam 'Idu, Muhammad. "Intafa'a Siraj Abu Bakr 'Martin Lings'" (2005CE/1909AH), Retrieved from the cultural forum: http://www.almultaka.net/makalat.php?subaction=showfull&id=1117481 536&archive=&start_from=&ucat=3&

* محيي الدين بن عربي، ذخائر الأعلاق: شرح ترجمان الأشواق، منشورات محمد علي بيضون، دار الكتب العلمية، بيروت – لبنان- ط١(١٤٢٠هـ/٢٠٠٠م)

* Ibn 'Arabi, Muhyi ad-Din. *Dhakha'ir al-A'laq: Sharh Tarjuman al-Ashwaq*, leaflets of Muhammad Ali Baydoun, Dar al-'Ilmiyya, Lebanon: Beirut. 1st edition (2000CE/1420AH).

* ملك مصطفى ، "مسجد في قلب الحي الاندلسي العتيق بعد ٥٠٠ عام من الصمت – من ينفض الغبار عن الثقافة الاسلامية في إسبانيا" جريدة (الزمان) – العدد ١٥٦١ – التّاريخ ٢٠/٠٧/٢٠٠٣.

* Malak, Mustafa. "Masjid fi Qalbi al-Hayyi al-Andalusiyyi al-'Atiq Ba'da 500 'Am Mina as-Samt: Man Yanfudu al-Ghubbar 'An ath-Thaqafati al-Islamiyyati fi Isbaniya", in: az-Zaman Magazine. N.1561 (July 20, 2003).

* نهاد خياطة، "رينيه غينون والمنقول الحقيقي" تم تصفحه يوم: ١٠/٠٨/٢٠٠٧ على : http://maaber.50megs.com/issue_february06/spiritual_traditions2.htm#_ftn2

* Khayyata, Nihad. "René Guénon wa al-Manqul al-Haqiqi", Retrieved in August 10, 2007. from: http://maaber.50megs.com/issue_february06/spiritual_traditions2.htm#_ftn2
* Hajji, Muhammad. "Moroccans Chose Moderate Sufism", interviewed by: Al-Ishara Newspaper, 2nd year, Volume N.16 (April: 2001).

2. ENGLISH BIBLIOGRAPHY

* Abdaqadir as-Sufi, *Root Islamic Education*, Ch.1. On-line at: http://bewley.virtualave.net Viewed July 2007
* Abdalqadir As-Sufi, *Technique of the Coup de Banque*, on website: http://66.49.205.6/books/Coupdebanque.pdf.
* Abdul Wahab el-Affendi, "A False Dawn" in: Inquiry Magazine (January 1998).
* Andrew Rawlinson "A History of Western Sufism" Diskus vol (1) no (1) 1993.
* Alan Godlas "Sufism, the West, and Modernity" in website: http://www.uga.edu/islam/sufismwest.html
* 'Ali al-Jamal al-'Amrani, *The Meaning of Man: The Foundations of the Science of Knowledge*, translated by: Aisha 'Abd ar-Rahman at-Tarjumana from the original text edited by: 'Abd al-Kabir al-Munawwar, Diwan Press, England (1977)
* 'Ali Kose, *Conversion to Islam: A study of Native British Converts*. London: Kegan Paul, (1996)
* Angela Alt, "An Open Letter on Sufism" in The Sufi, vol. 1, September 1934
* David Westerlund, *Sufism in Europe and North America*, David Westerlund (ed.) – Routledge Curson – London &New York, (2004)
* Fadhlallah Haeri, *Songs of Iman on the Roads of Pakistan: Talks Given During a Tour of Pakistan*, Zahra Publications, Blanco, TX, U.S. A, (1983)
* Frithjof Schuon, *The Transcendent Unity of Religions*, Translated by: Peter Townsend, Harper & Row (1975)
* Frithjof Schuon, *Islam and the Perennial Philosophy*, Translated by: J.Peter Hobson, Preface by: Seyyed Hossein Nasr, World of Islam

Festival Company Ltd, (1976)
* Fuad Nahdi, "Introducing a Mountain" in: Q-News, n: 363, June (2005)
* GF Haddad, "The Murabitun & Shaykh Nazim al-Haqqani: Refutation of Umar Vadillo's The Esoteric Deviation in Islam in: http://www.sunnah.org/publication/salafi/vadillo/murabitun.htm
* Hamza Yusuf, "A Spiritual Giant In an Age of Dwarfed Terrestrial Aspirations" in: Q-News , n:363, June(2005)
* Ian Dallas, *Collected Works*, Budgate Press, Cape Town, (2005)
* Inayat Khan, *The Art of Being and Becoming*, New Lebanon, NY: Omega, (1982)
* Inayat Khan, *Biography of Pir-o-Murshid Inayat Khan* (1923), Germany: Centrum Universel, (2005)
* James Winston Morris, "Ibn 'Arabi in the 'Far West' Visible and Invisible Influences" in the Journal of the Muhyiddin Ibn 'Arabi Society, IX (2001)
* Marcia Hermansen, "In the Garden of American Sufi Movements: Hybrids and Perennials," in: New Trends and Developments in the World of Islam, ed. Peter Clarke, London: Luzac Oriental Press, (1997)
* Marcia Hermansen, "The 'Other' Shadhilis of the West" in The Shadhiliyya, ed. Eric Geoffroy, Paris: Maisonneuve et Larose, (2005)
* Mark Sedgwick, *Against the Modern World: Traditionalism and the Secret Intellectual History of the Twentieth Century*, Oxford University Press, (2004)
* Mark Sedgwick, "European Neo-Sufi Movements in the Interwar Period" in: *Islam in Europe in the Interwar Period: Networks, Status, Challenges*, Nathalie Clayer and Eric Germain, eds. Forthcoming London: Hurst.
* Mark Sedgwick "In Search of the Counter-Reformation: Anti-Sufi Stereotypes and the Budshishiyya's Response" in Charles Kurzman and Michael Browers, eds, *An Islamic Reformation?* Lanham, Md: Lexington Books, (2004)
* Mark Sedgwick "Traditionalist Sufism" in ARIES 22 (1999)
* Martin Lings, *A Sufi Saint of the Twentieth Century: Shaykh Ahmad Al-

Bibliography

Alawi His Spiritual Heritage and Legacy, ed.3, The Islamic Texts Society, Cambridge (1993)
* Martin Lings, *What Is Sufism?*, The Islamic Texts Society, Cambridge, UK, (1993)
* Martin Lings, "René Guénon" in: SOPHIA, vol. 1, No. 1 (summer 1995).
* Michael Fitzgerald, "In Memoriam: Dr.Martin Lings" in: "Vincit Omnia Veritas" II, 1
* Muhammad Ibn al-Habib, *The Diwan of Shaykh Ibn al-Habib*, Translated by Aisha Bewley, Madinah Press (2001)
* Nuh Ha Mim Keller, "Becoming Muslim" in: http://www.masud.co.uk/ISLAM/nuh/bmuslim.htm viewed: 10/08/2003
* Omar K. Neusser, "Defense against Slander and Takfir Coming from the 'Murabitun' Movement as an Example for Sects in General" in: http://www.livingislam.org/o/dstm_e.html viewed: 18/08/2007
* Peter Young, "Ibn 'Arabi: Towards a Universal Point of View" in the Journal of the Muhyiddin Ibn 'Arabi Society, V, (1999)
* Ron Geaves, *The Sufis of Britain: An Exploration of Muslim Identity*. (Cardiff: Cardiff Academic Press, 2000)
* Seyyed Hossein Nasr, "The Biography of Frithjof Schuon", in *Religion of the Heart* (essays presented to Frithjof Schuon on his Eightieth Birthday), edited by: Seyyed Hossein Nasr & William Stoddart, Foundation For Traditional Studies, Washington, D.C. (1991)
* Sophia, Journal of Traditional Studies, vol. 4, no. 2, Winter 1998, (dedicated to the memory of Frithjof Schuon)
* Stephen Schwartz, "The 'Sufi' Master of Deceit: Hamza Yusuf Hanson" viewed 25/08/2007 in: http://www.familysecuritymatters.org/global.php?id=881447
* Titus Burckhardt, *An Introduction To Sufism*, Translated by: D. M. Matheson, Thorsons an Imprint of Harper Collins Publishers, London (1995)
* Umar Ibrahim Vadillo, *The Esoteric Deviation in Islam*, Madinah Press, 1st Edition, (2002)
* Umar Ibrahim Vadillo, "Fatwa on Banking: And the Use of Interest Received on Bank Deposits" on webpage:

http://www.shaykhabdalqadir.com/content/articles/FatwaOnBanking.pdf viewed:10/08/2007
* William Stoddart, "Titus Burckhardt and the Perennialist School" in: http://religioperennis.org/documents/stoddart/TB.pdf viewed: 15/08/2007

3. FRENCH BIBLIOGRAPHY

* Erik Geoffroy, "Le Soufisme d'Occident dans le Miroir du Soufisme d'Orient" dans: Annales du Patrimoine, n.04, Septembre 2005
* Fatima Harrak, "Le Soufisme Face à La Mondialisation: Cas Des Confréries D'Origine Africaine Aux USA" dans: Confréries Soufis d'Afrique: Nouveaux Rôles, Nouveaux Enjeux, 2004, Actes du Colloque International, Organisé par l'Institut des Etudes Africaines Rabat, 2-4 Octobre (2001)
* Frithjof Schuon, *Comprendre l'Islam*, Editions du Seuil, Imprimerie Hérissey à Evreaux, (1976)
* Mark J. Sedgwick, *Le Soufisme*, Traduit de l'anglais par: Jean-François Mayer, Les Editions du Cerf, (2001)

4. WEBSITES

* http://www.almultaka.net/makalat.php?subaction=showfull&id=1 117481536&archive=&start_from=&ucat=3&
* http://bewley.virtualave.net
* http://maaber.50megs.com/issue_february06/spiritual_traditions2.htm#_ftn2
* http://www.alkhoei.org/?l=6&b=6&p=37&c=47
* http://www.islam-maroc.gov.ma/ar/detail.aspx?id=1619&z=14&s=1
* http://www.shaykhabdalqadir.com/content/books.html
* http://bewley.virtualave.net
* http://www.angelfire.com/ab2/bookwork/index.html
* http://www.shaykhabdalqadir.com/content/video.html
* http://ourworld.compuserve.com/homepages/ABewley/saq.html
* http://religioperennis.org/documents/stoddart/TB.pdf
* http://www.shaykhabdalqadir.com/content/articles/FatwaOnBanking.pdf
* http://www.familysecuritymatters.org/global.php?id=881447
* http://www.livingislam.org/o/dstm_e.htm
* http://www.masud.co.uk/ISLAM/nuh/bmuslim.htm
* http://www.sunnah.org/publication/salafi/vadillo/murabitun.htm
* http://www.uga.edu/islam/sufismwest.html
* http://66.49.205.6/books/Coupdebanque.pdf.
* http://sheikhhamza.com/biography_text.asp
* http://en.wikipedia.org/wiki/Hamza_Yusuf#_note-0
* http://en.wikipedia.org/wiki/Muhammad_ibn_al-Habib
* http://en.wikipedia.org/wiki/Muhammad_ibn_al-Habib
* http://www.sufiway.net/zawiya_birmingham.html

Bibliography

* http://www.sufiway.net/zawiya_london.html
* http://www.sufiway.net/zawiyabradford.html
* http://www.sufiway.net/znottingham.html